I0067375

## Praise for *The C'crets of Networking*

*"We all have been faced with the Coconuts and Cling-ons; Debbie Leonard's* C'crets of Networking *teaches you in a fun, upbeat way how to handle these people in a friendly manner, at all your networking events."*

**Debra Swearingen,**
**Market President—Kansas City**
**Lead Bank**

*"An educator by nature and a networking professional by day, Debbie brings together in simple terms and stories ways to develop business relationships through networking that work. Her C'crets encourage the beginner or the experienced pro to try things differently to accomplish their goals."*

**Vicki McGuire**
**Director of Business Development**
**Working Spaces, Inc.**

*"Debbie is a master networker whose practical approaches to networking will give you specific goals and strategies to help you stand out in a crowd and make the most of your networking time. I love her 'C' theme! It helps me to stay focused and not let those 'Coconuts' or 'Collegiates' prevent me from making the connections that I was meant to make! Her* C'crets of Networking *is a must read, and if you ever have the chance to hear Debbie speak about networking please don't pass it up! Lessons for life in business will definitely be learned!"*

**Tiffany Wallander**
**Director of Business Development**
**Syndeo**

*"Debbie breaks down the complexities of networking into simple, do-able steps, helping to defeat the sometimes overwhelming experience of networking, and offers the boost of confidence necessary to turn a networking opportunity into successful relationship-building and business development."*

**Beverly M. Weber, Shareholder**
**Martin, Leigh, Laws & Fritzlen, P.C.**

*"Debbie is innovative, creative, insightful and willing to help each and every person tackle their business issues. I have learned more from Debbie about networking than I have from any other source in my 20+ years in business!"*

**Paula Switzer Potter**
**Client Retention & Relationship Expert**
**Switzer Training Resources, Inc.**

*"Debbie's presentation on networking addresses real-life issues and adds a bit of comedy to the reality we experience. Debbie is not afraid of addressing the difficulties we each face, based either on our own fears or the fears we encounter in others. My team has learned to identify the behaviors Debbie describes in* The C'crets of Networking, *and to adjust their approach to maximize their networking success."*

**Monica Dahl, AVP**
**Business Banking Manager**
**ARVEST BANK, Greater Kansas City**

# *The* C'crets *of* Networking

# *The* C'crets *of* Networking

## A Guide to (Tactfully) Navigating Past the Castoffs and Toward the Champions

Debbie L. Leonard, CPA, MBA

Networking Queen Publications, LLC
Overland Park, Kansas

Published by Networking Queen Publications, LLC
www.networkingqueenpub.com

Edited by Amy Woods Butler, The Story Scribe, LLC
www.thestoryscribe.com

Cover design by Michael Morris,
Highlands Ranch, Colorado

ISBN 978-0615944081

*This book is for all the Champions who have encouraged me to share my networking secrets and have assisted me in bringing my passion to print,*

*and*

*for Jay, Matt, Zach, Josh and Hannah, thank you for your love and support through this amazing experience.*

# CONTENTS

# INTRODUCTION

I hope you picked up this book because you're ready to change your NOTworking events into NETworking opportunities! I assume you've made up your mind to attend networking events, so I won't try to convince you of the importance of networking. Instead, I will give you strategies to make your networking events the most productive they can be.

You won't find any "Networking Facts" in this book. What you will find is a systematic approach to networking that has been successful for me in the past. I've attended thousands of networking events over the past thirty years and I've mastered the art of networking. In that time, I've identified the characters you will consistently encounter, no matter how sophisticated the event or how frequently the group meets. Collectively, the participants at these events can be referred to as Contestants: like you, they are there to compete for the "best" networking encounters with the other attendees. While everyone starts off on equal footing as a **Contestant**, each soon falls into one of two camps: **Castoffs** or **Champions**. Through preparation and some careful observation you will learn to identify who are the Champions—those with whom you wish to build a relationship—and who are the Castoffs—those you're better off avoiding (at least at events).

♛♛♛

"*Wait a minute!*" you're probably thinking. "Aren't you a CPA? Why should I be interested in what you have to say about *networking*?" I understand. After all, as a Certified Public Accountant I'm part of a profession famously allergic to networking; if there's a list of the top five professionals who are the typical stand-outs at networking events, the CPAs are, well, pressed against the back wall counting them. We're usually not the ones commanding the attention of the crowd or handing out stacks of business cards. How do I know this? Because for a brief time, I was one of those standing against the wall, waiting for all the benefits of "networking" to miraculously kick in.

My introduction to the world of networking events began during my first big job with a large accounting firm immediately following my graduation from the University of Kansas. Then, as now, it was standard practice for new accountants at big firms to work like the dickens for ten years or so, then be rewarded with a "partner" title—along with the command to bring in new business. Unfortunately, many of these brand-new partners are poorly equipped for finding new clients. They may be motivated to attend networking events, and they may even have some minor successes in gaining a new client here or there, but generally the biggest gain is in their waistline—from too many networking drinks and dinners!

The last major firm I worked for had an interesting twist on networking. *All* the staff, not just the partners, were encouraged to attend networking events. Not only did the firm pay all the fees for the events, but as an incentive, non-partners received ten percent of any new business won! Well, I'm not one to let my advanced math classes go to waste; I did some figuring and realized that a ten percent commission was incentive enough to get me interested in networking!

*I mastered the 10-key calculator in two weeks*, I thought to myself, *how hard could this networking thing be?* With that thought, I bundled up all the confidence my twenty-six-year-old self could muster and walked into my first event—the grand opening of a new business with the Chamber of Commerce on hand to cut the ribbon. After the ceremony I followed everyone into the building, where a man with an official-looking name tag approached me.

"Enjoying yourself?" he asked. "Is there anything I can help you with?"

"Thank you," I said. "I'm here to get some new business!"

Mr. Official Name Tag laughed. "Well, that's getting to the point!"

I had no idea what type of event I was attending, or who would be in attendance. It turned out Mr. Official Name Tag was well on his way to building a Fortune 50 company, which has since grown into one of the largest employers in the Midwest. No, I didn't get a client that night, but I learned that I never wanted to be laughed at while I was being serious again.

At the next networking event, I sat back and observed. I answered when spoken to, but didn't make any attempts to start a conversation. It went like that until several events later when *it* happened: I exchanged my first business card (other than those given to family and friends!). It felt like a rite of passage, but I wasn't sure to what. I just knew that someone had given me her card, and I was thrilled! I went back to the office and taped it to the side of my big, fat, can-barely-get-my-arms-around-it monitor, where it stood on display for all to see: Vicki Mason, Accounting Supervisor.

Guess what? The next day, Vicki called and asked if she could bounce a couple tax questions off me. She was taking an evening tax class at the local university and was stuck on a problem. I was so excited she called I would have completed the whole assignment for her!

A day later I was at her office giving her a hand with some tax questions when the company controller walked by.

"Nice to meet you," Allison said after Vicki introduced us. "This is good timing, does your firm by chance do audits along with tax work?"

I did it! I networked! I couldn't wait for the next day. The audit partner and I called Allison and the next month I had a check in my hot little networking hands for $6,000! I was hooked. Not just because of the money—but for the rush that came from meeting someone new, helping them, and ultimately benefitting from the exchange myself. It was a win all around!

After that, I went to networking events as often as I could, and each time I tried something different. Sometimes my goal was to talk about a certain topic. Other times it was a competition with myself to talk to that one person in the crowd everyone was hanging around. That year I earned almost as much in commissions as I did in salary!

Not every event resulted in fireworks. I left many events discouraged, but never without thinking of something I could do differently next time.

I enjoyed networking and was so fortunate in gaining new business that after five years I decided to start my own firm. Now I was responsible for bringing in all the business! I attended literally every networking event I heard about, averaging twenty events a month for the first three months. After that, determined to make my networking as efficient as possible, I culled the number of networking groups to a select few and made sure to attend those regularly. I was determined to network efficiently and became extremely picky about which events to attend, making sure not to become a "repeat attender." (You know who they are: if there's an event, they show up. Their involvement is superficial at best, making it difficult to cultivate a relationship with them. They become the person that people refer to as "the gal I see at every event.")

I rehearsed in my head what I would say under certain circumstances or if I ran into certain people, a practice I still carry on today, and one of the fundamental pillars of the C'crets I am going to share with you.

## In Person Versus Online

A word about **FACE-to-FACE** networking versus **FACE-to-SPACE** networking: although social media is very useful in the preparation for networking in person, this book will *not* instruct you on how to network with online social media. While FACE-to-SPACE networking—via LinkedIn, Facebook, Twitter, or any of the countless other social media sites—is no longer an option but rather a necessity in today's business world, the best way to nurture a relationship with someone is still *in person*. Facial expressions, voice inflection and body language are an integral part of developing a relationship. No emoticon can convey the sincerity of your intentions or capture the spark of your passion the way you yourself can when meeting someone FACE-to-FACE.

♛♛♛

A reward for being a networking expert is the ability to share the techniques that have made me successful. Much of this I've shared as a frequent speaker at meetings, conventions and other gatherings. Through my many speaking engagements, I've learned that people retain information presented in a humorous or informal way, and that's what I have striven for in this book—and why all the C'crets and Characters start with the letter "C." Information delivered in patterns or through repetition increases retention; so does acting out or rehearsing situations. To that end, I've included short exercises that will help you brainstorm solutions to problems before they occur, so that when you find yourself face to face with a Contestant—whether a Castoff or a Champion—you'll be ready to act with confidence, verve and a high probability of success.

♛♛♛

The book is divided into four simple sections:

- ♛ **Section One**
  *Prepare.* Before you attend a specific event, do your homework. I'll instruct you on what to do and give specific examples of how to do it.

- ♛ **Section Two**
  *Recognize the Castoffs.* In order to get to the good stuff in networking, you have to navigate through the unproductive. I will teach you the C'crets of identifying the most common Castoffs and how to navigate around them—or avoid them altogether. For each Castoff, you'll see a Challenge Section with examples of exit scripts and tips on how to create your own escapes.

♛ **Section Three**
*Identify the Champions.* This is the fun part! I will teach you the C'crets to cultivating relationships with the type of people you want to meet, need to meet and *will* meet! Each C'cret comes with specific examples to help you put into practice what you've learned and start forming ties with your Champions.

♛ **Section Four**
*Put the C'crets into action!* After identifying your champions, what's next? Discover the seven essential C'crets that will increase your networking productivity and profitability!

That's it!

The C'crets of networking are laid here before you; it's my hope that your days of dreading networking will be left in the dust. And now, time to start your adventure into the *C'crets of Networking!*

**prepare** \pri-per\ verb: to put somebody or yourself into a suitable physical or mental state to do or experience something

# 1 Before the Event

Tony glanced at the clock on his cluttered desk and gave a start. It was later than he realized. As the publicist of a mid-sized graphic arts firm, he never minded staying late at work; it meant he had a few minutes of quiet time after the office emptied to get ready for the next day's grind. He laughed. At twenty-nine, he knew he was lucky that he had never thought of his job as a grind. To the contrary, growing the business from its fledgling days as part of the downtown incubator project had been Tony's passion for the past five years. When Joe, his old college roommate, approached him about a partnership, Tony didn't hesitate. It turned out his trust in Joe's entrepreneurial instincts had been well-founded: the company had doubled its revenue in each of the past three years. But a move to a new suite of offices meant the pressure to grow was even more acute, and Joe had been urging Tony to start attending more networking functions to increase the company's presence in the community. So far, he had shown up for two, but he couldn't really see the purpose of either. Tonight's event was to take place in the back room of one of his favorite bars; he couldn't quite remember the name of the group or exactly what time the event started, but at least he'd be able to have a drink and catch part of the game on the bar's jumbo t.v. Time to get a move on; a nagging feeling told him he was already late.

Like Tony, you may have been pressured by a co-worker or supervisor to beef up your networking activities. Or maybe you've heard about the benefits of successful networking from colleagues and decided to give it another go-around—despite poor results in the past. Whatever the reason, you've made the decision to attend a networking event. Good for you! Now, how do you ensure it *is* good for you? One word: **PREPARE**. Many people like Tony think that their preliminary work is done when they sign up for an event; all that's left to do is show up. Afterward, these same people can't understand why networking events never seem to live up to their promise. The missing key ingredient? **PREPARATION**. Preparing for an event is nearly as important as showing up for it, and a secret—one of the many C'crets you'll learn in this book—to turning a wasted opportunity into a fulfilled one.

Once you realize the starting line of a network event isn't the door leading into the event space, but rather your own computer screen days or even weeks in advance, you'll have a head start over other attendees, some of whom may be your business competitors. By following the suggestions presented in this chapter, you'll be prepared to make your networking experience both enjoyable *and* productive.

## Know Your Target Contacts

### *Step One: the Event Attendee List*

The advantage of obtaining an attendee list is HUGE! Seeing the attendee list *before* the event is even HUGER! Is that even a word?! It should be because in this case it's true. How many times have you attended an event and seen someone who looks familiar, but can't place him or remember his name? Preparation is the key for turning a "*deja vu*" into an "*I know you!*"

Getting your hands on the list ahead of time will help you map out your route. If networking is a roadmap—directing you where you want to go—the attendees are the "attractions." Some are worth a stop; others warrant a drive-by; and a few you'll want to detour around. Preparing with the attendee list will help you avoid stopping to ogle a large pothole in the road when the Grand Canyon is just around the bend!

♛♛♛

I'll talk in a moment about how to use the attendee list, but first, how do you get your hands on the list? Aside from participating on the event committee—something you may consider doing to further your involvement with a group—there are a few ways to go about it.

Often you'll find the list, or a link to it, on the same website used to register for the event. But even if it's not posted online, don't give up. Locate the name of one of the organizers—one easy way is to look for the person to whom the RSVPs are addressed—and send an email requesting the attendee list. For events using invitation websites such as Evite or Punchbowl, take advantage of the site's built-in options to see who plans on attending; as a bonus, these sites can automatically notify you each time someone new signs up.

Once you have the list, don't wait until the last minute to print it. The more time you have to go over it, the better! Because the list will grow as you approach the event date, be prepared to make additions as new names appear. Bookmark the web page where the list appears and check it every other day.

### *Step Two: Create a Contact List*

The next step after you've obtained the attendee list—even if it's just a partial list—is to turn it into an **Event Contact List.**

First, look over the names of the people and the companies they represent. Quite frequently the list will contain the following important information:

- **the attendee's full name** (sometimes a nickname is listed)
- **his or her company**
- **direct business email address**
- **company contact information**, such as a phone number and address

Take advantage of collecting this information while it's easily available; when you're at the event, you may not have the opportunity to obtain a business card from everyone. By putting in the effort to get the list ahead of time, you'll have access to everyone's contact information if you need it later.

### *Step Three: Identify Your Target Contacts*

Now that you've looked over the list, it's time to pull out your favorite pen and mark it up! **First, jot down a checkmark next to the names of people you already know**. These may be individuals you'd like to reconnect with, or simply friendly acquaintances.

**Next, put a star next to the people you'd like to meet: these are your target contacts.** There are many ways to determine who they should be: for example, your supervisor may have mentioned that he would love the opportunity to bid on a job for Company GHI. Scanning the list of attendees, you see that Bob Johnson from GHI is attending; Bob qualifies for a star next to his name! Another contact you may want to meet could be a person you find fascinating. I've attended several networking events where I just wanted to meet a professional who has written a book. Sometimes there will be an attendee you admire and would like the opportunity to learn from or work for.

Once you've completed assigning the stars and checkmarks, it's time to **choose no more than three starred attendees**. Ask yourself this question: if I can meet only three people at this event, who would I want them to be? Bouncing from person to person may work for cocktail parties, but it's not always effective for a networking event. By narrowing your focus to just three, you increase your chance of forging a strong contact with *exactly the people you want to meet* at the event.

Often there will be more than one attendee from a company; if it's a company of interest, like GHI, you may be tempted to make each a target contact. Instead, narrow your choices by looking at their job descriptions. Is it more important to initiate a networking relationship with Bob Johnson, the lead engineer on a project, or with Sally Adams, the purchasing agent? Making this distinction before you show up for an event

## *Sample Attendee List*

| Name | Company | Email | Phone | Address |
|---|---|---|---|---|
| ✱ Todd Albright | Growing Companies, Inc. | talby@ growcokc.com | 816-555-0909 | 316 Main St. |
| Sandy Karr | Blagget Industries | sandy@ blaggett.com | 816-555-5985 | 4747 Laclede |
| ✓ John Cole | Chompers Mfg. | jcole@ chompersmfg.com | 913-555-4200 | 1929 Galvin St. |
| ✓ Steve Robinson | Ace Motors | steve@ acemotorskc.com | 913-555-5309 | 2030 Abner Road |
| ✱ Barb Woods | Singleton Mutual | bcw@ singletonop.com | 913-555-0000 | 17 Plossom Blvd. |
| ✱ Glenn Bearded | Slugo Electronics | glennon@ slugoelectro.com | 913-555-8111 | 3567 Broadway |
| ✓ Cecilia Kaup | Learning Light | ckaup@ learninglight.org | 866-555-2389 | 8929 Northeast |
| Bob Zuehle | Big Jets, Inc. | rzuehle@ bigjetskc.com | 816-555-1717 | 1270 N. Skylark |

will maximize your time while there.

Meeting your targets is only the first step. Your goal after identifying your three target contacts is to plan a follow-up one-on-one meeting with each. Knowledge of the C'crets will help you accomplish this; without the C'crets, you will be depending on luck to meet even one target contact!

## The Contact Preparation Worksheet

The first step is to find out all you can about the target contacts you've identified. If a target contact has been on your wish list for awhile, chances are you've already gathered the information you need, but may not have it written down anywhere. If you are unfamiliar with a target, you have some preparation work ahead of you. To compile specific information on your three target contacts, I recommend you build a ***Contact Preparation Worksheet*** for each of your three target contacts.

### *Contact Details*

Let's start by identifying one of our target contacts by name and company. To illustrate, I'll create entries for the fictitious Todd Albright, owner of the imaginary Growing Companies, Inc.

Make sure you know the actual name of your target contact, not just his or her nickname. It's also imperative you have the correct spelling; one careless but easily avoidable mistake is to assume a name is spelled traditionally. Today, many names are modified versions of traditional favorites. My name, for example, is spelled Debbie. While Debby and Debi are just as common, it rubs me wrong—as it does most people—when someone addresses me in writing with the wrong version of my name. Let's face it: when someone doesn't take the time to verify the spelling of our name, it gives us the impression that he doesn't respect us. Everyone's name is a fundamental link to her identity; taking care to get that name right is the easiest way to give a good first impression!

## Contact Preparation Worksheet

Enter the target contact's name, company, phone number and any other pertinent information in the first column.

| Contact Name and Company | Company Information | What Can I Offer the Contact? | What Do I Want from the Contact? | Who Can Connect Me? |
|---|---|---|---|---|
| Todd Albright<br>Growing Companies, Inc.<br><br>816-555-0909<br>talby@growcokc.com<br><br>Headquartered in Kansas City<br><br>Startup: 2012 | | | | |

Regarding the company name, again, spelling is key. Consider the company Invision Technologies. The word "invision" is a play on the phrase "in sight." For example, the solution is "in sight." The word "envision," on the other hand, implies forward thinking. When pronounced, both words sound the same. A company named Envision may be a publication or marketing firm, but one called Invision is more likely to be a manufacturer of optical equipment, perhaps the photo eye sensors used on assembly lines. Contacting one when you want the other may get you interesting results, but probably not productive ones.

The company website may present another challenge. Generally, there are a few common top-level domains, such as .com, .org or .net. Using the wrong three little letters could cause you to look up the incorrect company, which can sometimes lead to embarrassing results, as I experienced first-hand several years ago: an organization in support of breast cancer awareness, "Back in the Swing," was raising money by selling a discount card honored by merchants in the Kansas City metropolitan area on one specific weekend in October. I purchased a card from a client, who told me I'd find a complete listing of participating merchants by going to the website www.backintheswing.com. When I typed in the website it directed me to a...well...swinger's site! After I stopped laughing, I called my client. It turned out the address she should have given me ended in ".org," not ".com!"

ICANN, the body governing naming rights on the internet, is preparing to unveil hundreds, if not thousands, of new top-level domains for purchase in the near future—everything from new country codes to company brand names. This will make it even more important to ask, rather than guess, a website's address.

Another possible pitfall involves confusing a *founder's* name with the *company* name. For example, in 1955, two brothers with the last name of Bloch founded a tax preparation company in Kansas City. When coming up with the company name, they started with each of their first initials, then altered the spelling of their last name from "Bloch" to its more recognizable homonym "Block." With that, they created the name "H&R Block." An astute correspondent would know to address a letter or email to Mr. Henry Bloch, not Mr. Henry Block.

These may seem like petty distinctions, but to the recipient, a misspelled name is anything but trivial.

### *By the Number*

Does the company have more than one location? If so, is the target contact located at headquarters or a branch location? Is there one phone number for all locations, with an extension number for your target contact, or does he have a direct dial number? Often employees working for companies with multiple locations are assigned email addresses with domain names specific to their branch. You don't want to send Bob Johnson a message addressed to bjohnson@ghi.com if his address uses the @ghi-us domain. You may have to do a little digging to find out this information, but it's worth the effort to make sure your future phone calls and emails reach your target contact.

There are bound to be companies on the list you've never heard of. Google them to see if they may be a fit for your services or product. In some cases, as you go through the attendee list you will discover new companies that are potential prospects. Some of the best companies to do business with are those that operate "under the radar." Their names may not be commonplace, but they are fantastic connections! Newer or low-profile companies are less likely to be over-solicited and more likely to be receptive to you. At the very least, being informed will give you a leg up when speaking one-on-one with the target contact.

### *Business Specifics*

Next, what do you know about the contact specifically? Identify pertinent information such as job title, responsibilities, length of time in the current position, and special skills. Do a web search for news articles relating to the company's operations or markets. Has the target contact or the company won any awards lately? Or any big contracts? Has either the contact or the company made any acquisitions or divestitures, or made the news for any positive reasons? What can you find out about the target contact specifically? How long has he been in his position? What can you find out about his responsibilities? Is he quoted in any articles that give you a clue to his focus or priorities regarding the business? This information will help you when you ultimately meet the contact.

Learning all you can about the target contact is the best preparation for meeting that person, but beware of crossing the line between constructive research and creepy inquiry. The last thing you want is for this person to "hear" you've been asking around about him! The best way to avoid crossing the creepy line is to limit your inquiries to online public information.

In the second column of the Contact Preparation Worksheet, create bullet points for facts about the company, including items about the target contact's role within the company. (If it's a relatively new enterprise, like the one in our example, information may be limited.)

## Contact Preparation Worksheet

Enter the details about the target contact's job responsibilities and general company information in the second column.

| Contact Name and Company | Company Information | What Can I Offer the Contact? | What Do I Want from the Contact? | Who Can Connect Me? |
|---|---|---|---|---|
| Todd Albright<br>Growing Companies, Inc.<br><br>816-555-0909<br>talby@growcokc.com<br><br>Headquartered in Kansas City<br><br>Startup: 2012 | • Financial Officer (new)<br>• Acquisition mode<br>• Small accounting dept.<br>• responsible for many functions, spread thin | | | |

### *What Can You Offer the Target Contact?*

Here's one C'cret of networking worth remembering—it is better to give than to receive. If you're looking exclusively at the benefits a contact can provide you without giving a thought to his needs, you won't get far. Networking relationships must be mutually beneficial to be successful. When determining your target contacts, always be prepared to provide information, referrals or opportunities—rather than just asking for them. Then decide what you have to offer the contact *specifically*.

Usually, this falls into one of two categories. One, you may be a good resource for the target contact, or two, you may be able to provide specific business services or products that will help your target contact or his company.

Ideally, your bullet points should reveal what you can potentially offer the target contact. In our example, I could offer both services and connections. For instance, since I know that the company has a small accounting department, I could offer Mr. Albright connections to potential employees for positions he may need to fill.

The information I've gathered also reveals several ways I could make Mr. Albright's job easier with my services. If I hadn't done my homework, I might have met him at the event, suggested a future get-together for coffee, then promptly been shot down. Way, *way* down: Mr. Albright isn't the kind to have time for a leisurely coffee at the local coffee shop. Knowing his time is most likely very limited, I can plan my approach for an appointment in a way that will relieve some of his stress, rather than adding to it by becoming one more thing he has to manage. Based on this reasoning, I offer to bring coffee to his office to discuss some suggestions I have for blending the accounting procedures after the impending acquisition. His response? A big thumbs up and a smile of relief. By taking the time to learn

## Contact Preparation Worksheet

In the third column, enter specific ways in which you can help the target contact.

| Contact Name and Company | Company Information | What Can I Offer the Contact? | What Do I Want from the Contact? | Who Can Connect Me? |
|---|---|---|---|---|
| Todd Albright<br>Growing Companies, Inc.<br><br>816-555-0909<br>talby@growcokc.com<br><br>Headquartered in Kansas City<br><br>Startup: 2012 | • Financial Officer (new)<br>• Acquisition mode<br>• Small accounting dept.<br>• responsible for many functions, spread thin | • Experience in helping companies grow<br>• Perform temp. Controller functions<br>• Interview potential Controllers<br>• Help put procedures into place<br>• Make his job easier!! | | |

about my target contact, I'm able to offer what he needs in a way that benefits us both—a surefire method of generating a positive response.

Review your bullet point information and determine three or four items you can offer the target contact. Enter these in the third column of the Worksheet.

### *What Can the Target Contact Offer You?*

Your target contact may ask how you can benefit from a relationship with him; it's crucial to your networking success to have an answer. Too many people wander through networking events knowing *whom* they want to meet, but without a clear idea of *why*. If you don't know what you want, you probably won't get it.

Identify exactly why this person is on your contact list. Is the target contact someone you admire and want to learn from? Do you want to become a customer of the target contact? Do you want this person to become one of your customers? It's important to be specific about how the target contact can help you. Remember when I went to my first networking event? I told Mr. Official Name Tag, "I'm here to get some new business." If this scenario happened today, I would be more specific: "I would like to be introduced to a growing company in need of higher-level accounting support."

There is a lot to be said for getting that proverbial foot in the door. The remainder of the body will soon follow the foot, and before you know it, you are all the way in the door!

In the fourth column, list what you would like to gain from the target contact.

## Contact Preparation Worksheet

In the fourth column, enter specific ways in which the target contact can help you.

| Contact Name and Company | Company Information | What Can I Offer the Contact? | What Do I Want from the Contact? | Who Can Connect Me? |
|---|---|---|---|---|
| Todd Albright<br>Growing Companies, Inc.<br><br>816-555-0909<br>talby@growcokc.com<br><br>Headquartered in Kansas City<br><br>Startup: 2012 | • Financial Officer (new)<br>• Acquisition mode<br>• Small accounting dept.<br>• responsible for many functions, spread thin | • Experience in helping companies grow<br>• Perform temp. Controller functions<br>• Interview potential Controllers<br>• Help put procedures into place<br>• Make his job easier!! | • Relationship with a growing, influential company<br>• Ongoing supplemental accounting help and tax planning engagement<br>• Opportunity to assist in interesting transactions | |

### *Finding the Connection*

Before we complete the worksheet, let's go back to our original target contact list. We put a checkmark next to people we already know, but how about the people we haven't yet met but would like to?

Are there people you know who may be connected to those you would like to meet? List those people in the last column of our Contact Preparation Worksheet.

You won't always know someone in common with your target contact; in that case, you'll have to think of other ways to gain an introduction. One scenario may look like this: I notice that Todd Albright from Growing Companies, Inc. will be attending the event tonight. This company has been on my radar for several months; I have a target contact name, but how do I meet this person?

Most events will have the attendee name tags spread out alphabetically on the registration table. After selecting my name tag, I quickly peruse the rest and determine that Todd Albright—I have no idea what he looks like—has already checked in and picked up his name tag. I lean in to the person handling registration and say, "I could really use your help. I came to this event hoping to meet Todd Albright, and I notice he's already picked up his name tag. Would you be able to point him out to me?" If I do it right, it won't seem creepy and I most likely won't be escorted out of the event and slapped with a restraining order!

It's also a good idea to know whether the event is a "mixer," with no specific seating, or whether it's an event where you're expected to sit for the program or meal. If it is a seated event, you may want to get there early in order to be able to sit by the people you have targeted. It's human nature to want to be where things are familiar, and you'll naturally gravitate toward

## Contact Preparation Worksheet

In the fifth column, enter the name(s) of people who may be able to introduce you to your target contact.

| Contact Name and Company | Company Information | What Can I Offer the Contact? | What Do I Want from the Contact? | Who Can Connect Me? |
|---|---|---|---|---|
| Todd Albright<br>Growing Companies, Inc.<br><br>816-555-0909<br>talby@growcokc.com<br><br>Headquartered in Kansas City<br><br>Startup: 2012 | • Financial Officer (new)<br>• Acquisition mode<br>• Small accounting dept.<br>• responsible for many functions, spread thin | • Experience in helping companies grow<br>• Perform temp. Controller functions<br>• Interview potential Controllers<br>• Help put procedures into place<br>• Make his job easier!! | • Relationship with a growing, influential company<br>• Ongoing supplemental accounting help and tax planning engagement<br>• Opportunity to assist in interesting transactions | John Cole, LinkedIn |

those people you already know. Resist the temptation to do this! Instead, remind yourself that you are at the event to meet new people and make new connections.

## Know the When and Where and What's Appropriate

Last month, I received an email offer for a special deal on an oil change from a national chain of lube shops. In order to get the discounted price, I was instructed to visit their website, fill out some information, and select my appointment time. It was a great deal, so I didn't mind going through these steps.

Later that day I headed to the nearby shop, armed with the coupon I printed; I was even five minutes early for my appointment! It wasn't until after I pulled my car into the bay that I learned the coupon was valid not at that location, but one several miles across town. Because I always go to the same location, I hadn't bothered to check the address listed on the coupon—I didn't give it a second thought. I knew the WHEN, but not the WHERE of my appointment. Because I couldn't make it in time to the other shop, I stayed where I was, paid full price, and left feeling disappointed.

Knowing the event details of networking—the when, where and what's appropriate—is a basic prerequisite for success. I call these elements the Composition; before you attend an event, it is imperative to understand its Composition.

Knowing where and when may seem obvious, but often it's not; some events take place at the same venue every month, while other groups, in order to keep the atmosphere fresh, change venues after every three or four meetings.

Many times when registering for an event, it's tempting to skip over the question asking for your email. Filling it in will just get you on the event sponsor's email list, and who needs more emails every day? *You do*, if that email is going to notify you of last-minute event changes. Skipping the email question could cost you time, frustration and embarrassment if the Composition of the event has been changed.

As I mentioned, I do several speaking engagements throughout the year. A few days prior to my speaking engagements I always call to verify the location. Oftentimes the company I am speaking to has multiple locations. I never assume I know which location is hosting my presentation—assuming will almost always cause havoc! *Always double-check the location and time of the event you are attending.*

### *Dress for the Event*

Composition also involves being aware of the appropriate attire for the event. Try not to be the person who stands out—either for dressing up or dressing down. You may favor spaghetti strap blouses with a linen skirt, or khaki pants with a white tee shirt and sport jacket, but if the protocol calls for business attire, follow it. Likewise, some evening events may require cocktail dresses and jackets and ties. Don't try to make a fashion statement—or show your rebellious side!—at a networking event. You want to be remembered for your congeniality, not your clothing. *Know the protocol for dress attire and stick to it.*

### *Color*

While we are discussing clothing, let's take a quick detour and talk about color. Certain colors, like certain clothing styles, create different impressions. For example, the color red is considered a power color. Men will often wear red ties to meetings and networking events, and women may wear a dark suit or slacks with a red blouse. Darker colors imply authority, which is different from power. In general, power is more approachable than authority. We are drawn to powerful people.

The colors orange, pink, blue and green give a first impression of creativity. If you choose one of these colors, don't overdo it. Limit the color to a blouse, scarf, belt or accessories. Too much color is another way of dressing inappropriately; it draws attention to you in an undesirable way.

Oversized or excessive jewelry, unusual hairdos, visible tattoos or stiletto heels may be the style and make you look and feel stunning, but as with color, be careful with these accessories, as they will shift the focus away from what you are saying to what your are wearing.

## *Your most important accessory: the name tag*

At the registration desk, Adam scans the rows of name tags until he finds the one printed with his name. The clear plastic tag has a safety pin on the back; as he picks it up, he remembers that he left his suit jacket in the car. He'll have to pin it to his dress shirt. But today he's wearing his favorite pale blue striped shirt, and he remembers that the last time he pinned a name badge directly on a dress shirt it left a noticeable hole in the fabric. Rather than risk it, he forgoes wearing the name badge. He has his business cards, after all.

Adam's eyes scour the room for familiar faces. By the bar, he sees Blake Levine, a broker he met at a networking event a few weeks back. He meant to follow up with a one-on-one meeting but never got around to setting it up. Wow, he thinks, what great luck to run into him here! He walks over to Blake, who is talking to a small group of men.

"Hello Blake, nice to see you again!" says Adam with a big smile.

"You, too," replies Blake, a look of confusion on his face.

"I've been wanting to follow up with you about our last conversation." Adam launches into a talk about some marketing ideas they had discussed a few weeks ago, but Blake stops him abruptly and says he needs to speak with a woman across the room.

Knowing there's no way he'll remember the name of this guy—why isn't he wearing a name tag?!—Blake makes a quick, uncomfortable escape, and avoids Adam for the rest of the evening.

*Everyone* should wear a name tag at a networking event. Consider it a service to others; if they're preoccupied with trying to remember your name, you can be sure they're not paying attention to the conversation.

The best thing is to have a permanent name tag of your own. If you leave it up to the event staff, there's a good chance that your name or company name may be misspelled, the wrong name printed on the name tag, or most likely, the cheap name tag sticker will come unstuck and end up on the floor (name side up, of course!) for all to step on.

Invest in a permanent name tag and personalize it to convey who you are and what you do. For example, Mark Devereau of Devereau's Consulting Services lists both his name and company name on his badge, which elicits lots of questions about what type of consulting he does. This is positive and encourages conversation. After a few networking events, he decided to take it further, and ordered a name tag that read:

Mark Devereau
Devereau Consulting Services
"Ask me how to successfully
navigate Obamacare!"

At his next event, nearly everyone he met noticed the buzzword "Obamacare" and made a comment—some good, and some bad. Not only did it generate conversation, it made Mark more memorable to the people he spoke with.

Name tags may be the first impression you give a prospect, so make sure it's a memorable one!

## Castoffs vs Champions

As I mentioned in the outline, in order to get to the good stuff in networking, you have to navigate through the unproductive! People who impede your productive networking are your CASTOFFS. Castoffs will drain your energy and waste your valuable networking time. It's important to be able to identify the most common Castoffs and learn how to navigate around them or avoid them altogether!

CHAMPIONS, on the other hand, are those you meet who are excellent connectors of people! It's important to nurture your relationships with the Champions. You'll know you've found a true Champion when someone has a positive effect on your business and keeps your best interest in mind. Champions come by their name honestly: they will champion you *and* your business.

♛♛♛

Now that we've sliced and diced the attendee list a dozen ways, and learned the do's and don'ts about preparing for an event—let's put this hard work into action!

**castoff** \kast-ȯf\ noun: somebody or something that has been rejected or abandoned because no longer considered useful or attractive

# 2
# The Castoffs

Rachel's fingers fly across the keyboard of her computer. She's trying to get a couple more emails answered before heading out to a networking event at the new hotel downtown. She's been looking forward to this event for weeks; she has attended plenty of networking events since graduating from college in the spring, but this is the first to take place downtown, where she hopes to eventually work. Rachel adores the urban architecture, and feels a thrill whenever she sees the clusters of high-rise buildings.

Driving downtown, she reviews the attendee list in her mind. There are a couple people she is determined to meet, and she carefully rehearses in her mind what she wants to say. As she pulls open the door, a surge of confidence courses through her, and she practically skips into the event space. She's going to do great!

"Raaachel!" she hears a voice call out. "Rachel! Over here!"

Rachel would know that voice anywhere. She looks around, spots Haley Anderson, and gives a quick wave before darting deeper into the crowd. Rachel has nothing against Haley, whom she knows from college, but Haley tends to attach herself to Rachel at these events, either tagging along at her side or continually pulling her over to introduce her to people she "*has to meet!*" In the past, this has meant there was no time to connect with the people she really *wanted* to meet.

Across the room near the buffet table, Rachel spots Henry Eads, one of her target contacts. Just as she heads his way, Haley pops in front of her.

"Whew! I didn't think I'd ever catch up to you in this crowd!"

Rachel sighs and gives a last look at Henry. Downtown or not, this event is going to be a bust, like so many others. She quietly gives in as Haley takes her by the elbow and firmly leads her in the other direction. "I see my neighbor," Haley says. "I can't wait to introduce you—you're going to love her!"

## Who Are the Castoffs and Why Should I Avoid Them?

It's ironic that we will now devote a great deal of time discussing Castoffs, the very people we do *not* want to meet. But because unproductive relationships are time-consuming and lead us astray from our real goals, it's important to recognize the Castoffs and develop a plan for dealing with them. In this chapter, I'll describe the various types of Castoffs and help you spot them as easily as if they were wearing neon warning lights! And since I don't do things halfway, I'll provide guidance on how to handle them; identifying the Castoffs is meaningless unless you learn to deal decisively and effectively with them. That means making your exit before the Castoff ensnares you in a lengthy conversation.

At the end of each section, you'll find a list of "Challenges" to provide tips on how to deal with various situations and to encourage you to come up with your own "script." By preparing and rehearsing these scripts, you'll not only reduce the anxiety caused by interacting with these characters, you'll also avoid wasting time in fruitless conversation and free yourself to focus on building relationships with your Champions.

A bonus benefit of mastering Castoff recognition is that you will be more cognizant of your *own* actions; any of the Castoff tendencies you have will soon disappear! All of us slip up and "pull a Castoff move" now and then. The ability to recognize the move and stop yourself before it happens will be priceless in your networking endeavors!

Ready to get started? I would tell you to close your eyes and visualize, but that isn't practical while reading...so...put your imagination blinders on, and let's begin!

♛♛♛

We enter the networking event and look around, sizing up all the Contestants. (Remember, all attendees are Contestants until they've proven themselves to be a Castoff or Champion.) As the large group mills about, a low thrum of conversation fills the air. At first, the crowd doesn't look much different from that at last week's networking event. Slowly, though, as you glance around, you start to notice a few guests who stand out, and not in a good way...

There are certain people who waste no time in presenting themselves as Castoffs, as if they want to leave no question in your mind what kind of networker they are. I've identified three *obvious* Castoffs.

### *Castoff # 1: The Collagen*

This is the person who is constantly injecting BS into the conversation! You may have only just met this person, but the blathering takes on a life of its own and greets you like a pair of lips that have been injected with collagen one too many times!

The best course of action is to refrain from responding at all. Don't ask follow-up questions or say anything to encourage the Collagen. Don't let the giant lips suck you into a conversation! Resist the urge to laugh at all of his BS, as most Collagens will mistake this response for interest. Then, you need to turn around and run!

Realistically, you may not be able to run (or resist laughing!). In that case, what should you do? Let's look at an example.

**Collagen:** *Hello there, Debbie. I'm Dan Mathers. I couldn't help but notice your name tag says you're a CPA. What a stroke of luck for both of us! It just so happens I'm looking for a new CPA because I'm outgrowing my old one. Business is booming! I've got two major big box retailers who both want to carry the mattress my company makes, I'm planning to expand into three more states, and people are knocking down my door trying to get me to hire them because I run such a great company.*

**Debbie (trying to say as little as possible):** *Yes, I'm a CPA.*

**Collagen (not noticing the curt response):** *I'm also thinking of franchising…*

**Debbie (by now I have tuned out, and possibly tried body language to discourage further conversation):** *Well, it seems you have a lot going on. Good luck with that.*

With that, I turn and walk away.

Now, some may say I walked away from a potential new client. I did not. Two things clued me to the potential problems of having Dan Mathers as my client. First of all, saying so much about his business to a total stranger is a big warning sign—of immaturity, and most likely of a fabricated story. Second, he spoke of working on two steps momentous to any company: franchising and big box distribution. This is a lot of confidential information to be spewing forth to a stranger. From this brief discussion, I determined all his big talk was just an attempt to impress.

You will have to determine the degree of BS you can tolerate, but I strongly caution you against investing too much time with the Collagen.

### *Castoff #2: The Coconut*

Unlike the Collagen, the Coconut isn't out to impress; as a matter of fact, he doesn't even register the reaction he evokes when he suddenly drops into the middle of a conversation and utters something jarringly off-topic, bringing all talk to a screeching halt. Your best bet to get the conversation back in its groove? Be on the ready with a transitional comment. Here's an illustration to give you an idea of how it works:

**Henry (who has been enjoying a conversation with Diana for the past several minutes):** *I think it's fabulous that Frank is making such big strides! It's so unusual for…*

**Coconut: (stepping between Henry and Diana):** *Hiya, Henry! Did you catch that meteor shower last night?*

Henry now finds himself in an awkward position, with three choices. He can end his conversation with Diana; he can introduce the Coconut to Diana and include him in their conversation; or he can do what he really wants to do, which is to exclude the Coconut and continue his conversation with Diana.

**Henry picks the last option:** *I'm in the middle of a conversation with Diana. I'll catch up with you in a bit, okay?*

Henry then turns his body towards Diana, positioning his back towards the Coconut. If he did not turn his back on him, chances are the Coconut will stand there waiting for Henry to finish his conversation. Using body language, Henry sends the message that he is not going to engage the Coconut in conversation anytime soon. Faced with Henry's back, the Coconut will most likely move on and drop into someone else's conversation.

This type of behavior is immature and not appropriate for networking events. Henry wins Diana's appreciation for his expert handling of the situation: with just a few words and a simple body movement, he has smoothed over the interruption and put the conversation back on track. What Henry needs to keep in mind is that by "cracking" the Coconut and not letting him interrupt, he is not embarrassing or being rude to the Coconut in the least. Coconuts generally do not realize they are interrupting so they are rarely offended.

### *Castoff #3: The Cucumber*

The Cucumber is one of those people immediately recognizable: he's the one who is too cool to talk to you or anyone else at the event. He may add a few words to the conversation, but while he does so he continuously scans the crowd, looking for a companion more interesting than you. Or, he keeps a constant eye on his phone, monitoring it like it's the batphone about to start glowing with an important message from Gotham City! He may look at you with his cool, practiced faux smile. Remember the saying "cool as a cucumber?" The part you haven't heard is "a cool cucumber is just a couple days away from turning to mush!"

Another characteristic of Cucumbers is to put down the event they are attending. They may say something to you as if in confidence, such as "This event is never put together very well. I think it's a waste of time." So how do you respond?

One option is to respond in a snarky manner: "Then why are you here again?" Or you could play along and say, "I wonder who is in charge of this event? I bet they were understaffed or could use some fresh ideas. I may check into it." That will (or should) stifle the Cucumber because now you have taken some ownership of the event and any other comments would be a direct insult to you. It's not to say the Cucumber won't continue to utter inappropriate comments, but if he does, it will tip you off that the "mush" has set in and you should exit the conversation!

Unless the Cucumber was dragged forcefully to the event, he is there by choice and has no reason to "turn on the cool." Chances are good there isn't much substance to this person. If you really want to develop a relationship with the Cucumber, it may be best to attempt it outside of an event, where there are fewer distractions.

## Challenges

**Part I:** Think about the last several networking events you have attended. Fill in the name or a description of real people you have encountered who fit the categories below.

**Collagen** ______________________________

______________________________

______________________________

______________________________

______________________________

______________________________

**Coconut** ______________________________

______________________________

______________________________

______________________________

______________________________

______________________________

**Cucumber** ______________________________________

______________________________________

______________________________________

______________________________________

______________________________________

______________________________________

**Part II:** It helps to have some rehearsed scripts you're comfortable with for future encounters with Castoffs. Prepare a script for an "escape plan" based on your experience with the people you listed above, and practice these scripts before going to your next event. Here are some suggestions to get you started.

## Collagen

*A Collagen has cornered you; you see the lips moving but you don't believe a word coming out. Try interrupting the Collagen by saying, "Wow, you are so (interesting, educated, experienced...) I can't possibly add anything to this conversation. I'm going to find a conversation more my speed!" Then immediately turn and walk away.*

*Use the following lines to brainstorm other possible scenarios.*

**My Script Idea ♛ Collagen:** ____________________

____________________________________________

____________________________________________

____________________________________________

____________________________________________

____________________________________________

## Coconut

*Imagine you are having a really good conversation with someone you've just met. Just then a Coconut drops in and says something that brings the conversation to a halt. Instead of being speechless yourself, you could say, "Well, that was unexpected!" Turn away from the Coconut and continue with your original conversation.*

**My Script Idea ♛ Coconut:** ____________________

____________________________________________

____________________________________________

____________________________________________

____________________________________________

____________________________________________

## Cucumber

*This is the easiest escape. Let's say you're trying to talk to someone who seems to be looking straight at you, but then you realize she is really looking behind you or over your shoulder. If her attention continues to wander, simply say "I can see you are expecting a (call, visitor, etc...). I won't take up any more of your time!" Then turn and walk away. It is important to immediately walk away or the Cucumber will try to convince you to stay by saying, "Oh, no, I'm not expecting anyone." Then after giving you a moment of attention, she'll turn right back to mush.*

**My Script Idea ♛ Cucumber:**____________________

________________________________________

________________________________________

________________________________________

________________________________________

________________________________________

♛♛♛

Now you've learned to navigate past the *obvious* Castoffs, but you aren't in the clear yet! There's another group of Castoffs a little harder to recognize. They may not be as conspicuous as the first three, but they just as surely will sabotage your networking goals.

### *Castoff #4: The Coupon*

You are talking to a prospective client when someone walks over, greets you heartily, then recommends your services or products in glowing terms. Sounds good, right? Not so fast! The Coupon tells everyone how great a job you do, and you stand a little taller. Then, the next thing out of his mouth is some version of this: "And you wouldn't believe how cheap Christina's rates are!" or "Christina offers great discounts!" This is a form of price sabotage, and squashes any chance of charging a fair rate for your services or products. Some Coupons will go as far as quoting your fees to the prospect as part of their "recommendation." At this point you should clip the Coupon and say "Wow, I really should increase my fees! Thanks for reminding me." (And when you get back to your office—if possible—increase the Coupon's fees!)

The Coupon is damaging in several ways. We want to win customers based on our performance, integrity and product, and when someone praises our work and recognizes the qualities we strive for, it's like bubbles buoying up the conversation. These bubbles bolster our pride in what we do, and the value of it for anyone listening. But when the Coupon brings up pricing, these bubbles of affirmation start to pop, one by one, with every additional comment made. Whether done unintentionally or with a misguided notion of being "helpful," the Coupon's emphasis of price over quality diminishes the value of our work.

This can be a tough situation, as you don't want to discourage praise from existing customers. Perhaps you could pull the Coupon aside and tell him, "I appreciate your endorsement. I can't afford to give everyone the special pricing I give you. In the future, if you could leave out the fee part, it will keep me from having to raise all of my prices!"

### *Castoff #5: The Curious George*

The Curious George is the person who joins your conversation and begins to ask questions about your business. Sounds positive, huh? Generally the questions show a friendly interest, such as: how long have you been in business?, what is your specialty?, etc. The attention is energizing, you warm up to the new acquaintance, begin to wonder if this is someone who ought to be on your Champion list, and then...bam! Curious George pops a question or delivers a comment that reflects negatively on your business, industry or associates, and the conversation—and the mood—takes a swift turn down a dead-end street.

Here's an example: you're a general contractor in conversation with a small group of people, including one of your target contacts, a well-known commercial real estate developer.

Curious George wanders over and greets everyone with a smile. He turns to you and says, "I hear you're the general contractor on the new civic center. Congratulations!" The others offer their congratulations and ask a few questions about the new building, when Curious George, waiting for a pause in the conversation, says, "I hear general contractors cut corners on the big ticket items so they can come in on budget. I bet meeting budget on this project will earn you some good bonuses, huh?"

This really isn't so much a question, but rather a statement to provoke an argument or at the very least, one that puts you on the defensive. It's up to you to get the conversation back on a positive note. "We prefer to focus on OUR projects and track record of successes," you might say. Or you can turn the tables on Curious George by using his comment as a way to highlight the positives of your company: "Unfortunately, there are always those unscrupulous people who make the headlines. Thank goodness that's never been our way; our track record speaks for itself. We couldn't be happier to work on such a prestigious undertaking!" Inappropriate questions or comments make everyone uncomfortable. Continue the conversation with an upbeat attitude, which will not only show you have nothing to be defensive about, but will also take the air out of his argument. And everyone—with the exception of Curious George—will be relieved to have the conversation turned back to the positive.

### *Castoff #6: The Collegiate*

We all know this type of person from our school days: the social butterfly making her rounds, jumping into the party pic with you. Sure, we all like feeling like we belong to a group (that's what networking is all about, after all) but the Collegiate takes this to a new—and much more shallow—level. For one thing, she wants to be in every party pic! Whether taken by a professional photographer or just someone snapping shots on his cell phone, odds are these pictures will be published somewhere on a social media platform, and that's precisely why the Collegiate is eager to appear in them. But be wary of these unwanted photobombers. The activity may seem innocuous—a Collegiate will rarely waste your time by holding you hostage in profitless conversation—but there may be other negative consequences. If someone is, say, holding up a beer or a bottle of wine, sticking out her tongue, or making a rude hand gesture, when the photo is posted online it may create an impression of you—first or otherwise—that you don't want.

This scenario presents an interesting challenge, as you may not even be aware the picture is being taken until the flash goes off! The best you can hope for is advance warning from the party-pic taker or the hired paparazzi. If you see the Collegiate making the rounds with her camera, pull her aside and request not to be photographed. If that's not possible, take other precautions. For instance, if there are certain people you definitely do not want to appear next to in a photograph, it is your responsibility to stay away from them! Or if there is a photo you wish to be in, but prefer not to be shown holding an alcoholic drink, remember to set it down or otherwise keep it out of the frame of the photo. Murphy's law predicts that if you are speaking with a lady, and she hands you her drink while she is fishing in her purse for a business card (thereby leaving you holding a drink in each hand), the Collegiate will appear out of nowhere and take your picture!

If the Collegiate takes your picture after you've requested that she not do so, you may have no choice but to approach the host of the event and explain your dilemma. If you still don't get cooperation, leave the event.

## Challenges

**Part I:** Once again, think about the last several networking events you have attended. Describe the scenarios you've experienced where the following Castoffs have appeared. Try to remember how you responded. Writing it down will help you to avoid the awkwardness you felt in that situation the next time it happens. We will strategize some escape responses in Part II.

**Coupon**________________________________________

________________________________________________

________________________________________________

________________________________________________

________________________________________________

________________________________________________

**Curious George**__________________________________

________________________________________________

________________________________________________

________________________________________________

________________________________________________

________________________________________________

**Collegiate** ________________________________________

________________________________________________

________________________________________________

________________________________________________

________________________________________________

________________________________________________

**Part II:** Suggestions for YOUR escape. Read the suggestions below and come up with your own escape script.

## Coupon

*A glowing recommendation from a client ends with, "She is really inexpensive!"*

*One possible response: "Inexpensive is such a relative term. What he means is that I provide exemplary service for a very fair price. It's an important part of my philosophy."*

*Use the following lines to brainstorm other possible scenarios.*

**My Script Idea ♛ Coupon:** ______________________

______________________________________________

______________________________________________

______________________________________________

______________________________________________

______________________________________________

## Curious George

*When a question or comment addresses the quality of your work, or the integrity of your profession, respond in a way that doesn't sound defensive. One suggestion: "We value our repeat customers and feel they are our true testimonials."*

**My Script Idea ♛ Curious George:** ________________

______________________________________________

______________________________________________

______________________________________________

______________________________________________

______________________________________________

## Collegiate

*Picture this: you're having a lively conversation with a small group of people. Everyone is laughing and having a great time! All of a sudden the Collegiate, armed with a camera, swoops in for a photographic attack. You're holding a drink and do not want your picture taken, so you say politely, "No thank you, I'm not a picture person." If the Collegiate persists, turn away from the camera and feign a sneeze. Another alternative: put your hand across your face to ruin the picture! Remember, this is your image, and you have every right to decide where and when it will appear!*

**My Script Idea ♛ Collegiate:** ____________________

____________________________________________

____________________________________________

____________________________________________

____________________________________________

____________________________________________

♛♛♛

You've walked through the room and identified several Castoffs to steer clear of. Now, just when you think it's safe to continue, you run across three hopelessly helpful Castoffs. These Castoffs mean well, but their actions may be stifling or downright annoying.

### *Castoff #7: The Compass*

This may be someone you already know, or a new acquaintance who takes a fancy to you. Either way, the Compass is someone who insists on directing you around the room or event. She knows what you need, and won't let you stop her from giving it to you. There's no chance of you working the room as you wish with the Compass by your side. Her "helpfulness" is really a hinderance keeping you from reaching the people you'd like to meet. The Compass mistakenly believes it's her responsibility to introduce you to as many people as possible in the time allotted, and it becomes something of a contest to tally up the number of greetings. You've barely said hello to one person before the Compass is dragging you off to meet someone else.

How does the Compass become engaged with you? Maybe you said you were new to networking, or possibly mentioned you don't know many people at the event and hoped to be introduced to one or two new contacts. I call Compasses *helpful* Castoffs because they do not mean any harm or ill will at all. Quite the contrary! Yet, the methods they employ bring about the opposite result. There are times when nothing more than a brief introduction is appropriate, but in other instances, you'll want to extend the brief introduction into a more meaningful talk. Before you get the chance, however, the Compass is pointing you in the direction of the next special person you just "have to meet."

Sometimes what the Compass yearns for is the satisfaction of being "in the know." There are times when the Compass can be very helpful, if her powers are used for good, so to speak. Let's say that the Compass introduces you to Mr. Samuels, who cordially responds, "Nice to meet you," and nothing else. A ten-second silence ensues, which feels more like ten minutes. Thankfully, the Compass quickly directs you on to the next person!

Now let's look at the opposite scenario. The Compass introduces you to Ms. Merchants, the owner of a large retailer in town, who replies, "So nice to meet you. Your name sounds familiar, I wonder where we may have met before? Are you local?" This is a great segue into starting a conversation with Ms. Merchants, who has the potential to be a good network connection. As soon as the Compass hears, "So nice to meet you," she is tugging on your arm to move on to the next person. You have now missed your opportunity. Hopefully, when the Compass finally relinquishes you, you're able to go back to Ms. Merchants and salvage the situation. "I'm so happy you are still here. I wanted to make sure to finish our conversation. I've been thinking about where we may have met and I think it could be..."

Chances are Ms. Merchants recognizes that you were temporarily hijacked by a Compass and welcomes your return. If by chance Ms. Merchants comments on the Compass, it's best to brush it off without saying anything negative about the Compass, particularly since it's clear that her intentions are well-meaning. "Suzanne was very excited that I was able to attend today and I'm grateful for all the fabulous people she introduced me to."

### *Castoff #8: The Cling-on*

The opposite of the Compass, the Cling-on is someone you already know or just met who attaches herself to you like a kid hanging onto a security blanket. Instead of leading you around, she follows. As you introduce yourself to people, so does the Cling-on. We know that helping others is our first priority in developing relationships. The Cling-on takes this priority to a higher level by assuming ALL of your new introductions should be hers as well. By doing this, the Cling-on gives the impression that you are a team. The team could be co-workers, partners or simply friends that you endorse (or appear to endorse). This may not always be the impression you want to give someone you meet. Some people, when first introduced, find it awkward to have a one-on-one conversation with a "team" of two: two people approaching may cause intimidation or put the Target on the defensive. Depending on the situation and the people involved, it's generally counterproductive to try building meaningful relationships when you have another person in tow. Be helpful, but don't get stuck letting a Cling-on shadow you for an entire event.

### *Castoff #9: The Cheerleader*

The Cheerleader has energy to spare! She is always bubbly and jumps at the opportunity to sing your praises. In fact, she is so generous with compliments that others may start to doubt the sincerity of her words. The Cheerleader says things like, "Jen is fantastic with her customers! She knows so much about her products, she could write the catalog! Everyone loves her and her customers rave about her all the time! Customers drive out of their way to have Jen help them!" And so on...

The Cheerleader has only good intentions and wants to convey how awesome Jen is—but in the process it appears as if Jen "needs" all the praise, which dilutes the value of a sincere customer testimonial. Also, with all that fulsome praise, the Cheerleader tends to dominate the conversation, leaving little opportunity for Jen to speak for herself. The prospect would probably prefer to hear what Jen has to say for herself at some point.

One final point: it can be embarrassing to have someone go on about how great you are. The first compliment feels great, but by the third or fourth compliment, things can start get decidedly awkward. How do you halt the compliments without seeming as if you are interrupting or being ungrateful? Jen should shift the focus back to the prospect by injecting humor or simply ignoring all the over-the-top comments. She might say, "Wow! You make me sound so wonderful I may hire myself!"

## Challenges

**Part I:** Think back to the last several networking events you've attended. Describe scenarios you experienced where the following helpful Castoffs have appeared. Try to remember how you responded. We will strategize some escape responses in Part II.

**Compass** ______________________________________________

______________________________________________

______________________________________________

______________________________________________

______________________________________________

______________________________________________

**Cling-on** ______________________________________________

______________________________________________

______________________________________________

______________________________________________

______________________________________________

______________________________________________

**Cheerleader** ______________________________

______________________________

______________________________

______________________________

______________________________

______________________________

**Part II:** Suggestions for YOUR escape. Read the suggestions below and come up with your own escape script.

## Compass

*A well-meaning Compass is steering you around an event. She introduces you to Ms. Royal, with whom you quickly realize you'd like to have a longer chat. The Compass is pushing you to move on—what do you do?*

*One possible response is this: "Thank you so much for introducing me to Ms. Royal! I am lucky to have her ear for a few minutes, so I'm going to stay put, but I may catch up with you later!" Then turn back to Ms. Royal and continue your conversation. You need to make it clear that you are not inviting the Compass to stay and be a part of the conversation, which would encourage her to keep pulling you on to make the next introduction. Instead, you are subtly inviting the Compass to move on without you. This can be accomplished through body language by turning to separate yourself from the Compass.*

**My Script Idea ♛ Compass:** ______________________________

______________________________________________

______________________________________________

______________________________________________

______________________________________________

______________________________________________

## Cling-on

*The Cling-on is a little trickier to deal with than the Compass. This is because the Cling-on is not comfortable working the room on her own, and therefore will not "move on" quite so easily. You will have to look for an opportunity to let the Cling-on stand on her own without her, or the situation, feeling awkward. One possible scenario: when someone engages the Cling-on in a conversation, you say, "Will you two please excuse me for a moment? I want to catch so-and-so before he gets away!" While saying this, begin to MOVE away and KEEP going! By referring to the Cling-on and her new contact as "you two," you subliminally reinforce the concept of the two of them as a group unto themselves, increasing the chance they'll continue their conversation without any (or at least without much) awkwardness after your departure. You might also encourage the conversation by saying, "You two have a lot in common—I'll leave you to talk while I pop over to the bar for a minute." By encouraging the connection between them, you help the Cling-on gain confidence in her power to connect with others and at the same time free yourself to go meet someone else.*

**My Script Idea ♛ Cling-on:** ____________________

____________________________________________

____________________________________________

____________________________________________

____________________________________________

____________________________________________

## Cheerleader

*When the Cheerleader is on a roll, one of the easiest ways to head her off is to inject a little humor into the cheer! Let's say that Robin has been singing your praises and it is now on the downward spiral to becoming a bit ridiculous. Why not say, "Better stop now before my head gets too big for my tiara!" Other possibilities: "Thanks Robin, here's the $20 I promised you!"*

*My personal favorite, as I mentioned earlier, is, "Gee whiz! That sounded so good I think I will hire myself!"*

*Injecting humor will take the emphasis off what the Cheerleader has said and pull the conversation toward YOU. Your goal is to curb her overzealous praise and join the conversation in a more active way. Your Champions will appreciate your finesse at guiding the conversation onto another topic; not only does this improve the quality of the conversation, it will also reassure the others and put them at ease with you.*

**My Script Idea ♛ Cheerleader:** ______________________

______________________________________________

______________________________________________

______________________________________________

______________________________________________

______________________________________________

## Honorary Mention Castoffs

The only way to deal with the three following honorary mention Castoffs is to CUT and RUN! CUT and RUN allows you to stop the conversation, interaction or staring contest and move on! No exit strategies needed: get out however you can. Turn abruptly, quietly slip away, or excuse yourself to go to the restroom, the bar, to help the host or get some fresh air!

### *The Coil*

The Coil is one of those people so tightly wound that you're nervous just being around them. You aren't sure if they will explode or hug you; everything is an issue and a casual conversation is nearly impossible. Is this the type of person you want to spend your networking time on? By labeling Coils as honorary mention Castoffs, you're not cutting out the possibility of being cordial or even friendly with them; you just recognize that a networking event isn't the place to try to unwind them!

### *The Constipator*

The Constipator is the person always coming up with roadblocks, the one who clogs up the flow of energy. The Constipator comes in different forms. For example, he may be an employee at one of your target companies. "I'd like to meet your colleague, Mr. Austin," you mention in conversation with the Constipator. He immediately responds, "Mr. Austin is very busy and I don't think he would be interested." This is the first sign of a Constipator: he isn't willing to make an introduction or even suggest how to get your foot in the door. If this person were at the front desk of a company, he'd be called the "gatekeeper." Since he's a person of some authority representing his company at a networking event, well, he's no longer a gatekeeper, he's a *Constipator*.

### *The Cat*

The Cat is a little harder to read at first—you may have to spend some time with him before you recognize him as a Cat. With all due respect to feline lovers, the Cat—like his namesake—couldn't care less about you; his only concern is making sure you feed him! Cats are Castoffs who take and take, and never reciprocate.

So how do you recognize someone as a Cat, particularly if you've just met him, and haven't had any business dealings with him yet? It's easy. The Cat will dominate the conversation. He'll focus on himself and his work. He won't ask what he can do for you; he won't even ask WHAT you do. The Cat trains the spotlight on himself; it doesn't matter to him if you pay attention because he gets plenty of attention from himself.

It reminds me of a story I heard at a conference not long ago. A man had gotten into the habit of talking excessively about himself, his job and what he thought about everything he was doing. His wife pointed this out, and told him he was being "self-absorbed." Embarrassed, he thought it over, realized she was right, and decided to make a change. He apologized to his family and friends and pledged to be more considerate and attentive to others. Soon after, while he and his wife were out to dinner with a group of friends, he forgot his resolution and began to monopolize the conversation with stories about himself and his job. His wife gave him the "look" and he immediately took notice. He stopped in his tracks and said to the group, "Well, enough about what I think of my job. What do YOU think of it?"

This is a Cat! And what do you do with a Cat? You put him out! Let's face it, unless you smell like tunafish, a Cat couldn't care less about what you do or where you work!

**champion** \cham-pē-ən\ noun: **1** a defender, supporter, or promoter of somebody or something **2** a personal example of excellence or achievement

# 3
# The Champions

Cassandra is a principal in a prestigious architecture firm. She has been attending an annual real estate event for the past five years; each year there has been an amazing speaker, and this year promises to be the best!

As she pours a cup of coffee in the staff room, Cassandra thinks back to when she was the staff architect, fresh out of college. She wishes she had known which networking events to attend right from the start. She joined the architecture firm with six other associates and was lost in the crowd for the first two years. Then, almost by accident, she made her first real connection at a networking coffee: Cassandra was asked to work the registration desk at the monthly meeting of Women In Real Estate (WIRE), where she was given the task of arranging the name tags on the registration table. A simple task, but Cassandra decided to arrange the name tags in two pyramid shapes rather than in the normal rectangle with rows of tags. The first pyramid contained the tags for last names beginning with A – L. The second pyramid represented name tags for last names beginning with M – Z.

Lori Rayback, CDO (Chief Design Officer) of a large interior design firm, commented to Cassandra about the interesting layout of the name tags. Cassandra chuckled and said, "That's what happens when you leave a creative type in charge!"

An hour later, Cassandra found herself in a group of women discussing a hotel that recently opened for business. When the subject of furnishings came up,

Cassandra said, "The building is remarkable, both inside and out. But I would have picked more modern furniture to complement the sharp angles in the lobby."

Lori Rayback responded, "I totally agree. Let me guess, you must be either a designer or an architect, right?"

Cassandra smiled, "I'm an architect and a designer wanna-be! I really enjoy working with the designers on my projects and have managed to pick up a few pointers along the way!"

Lori smiled and said, "I'll have to show you some of the catalogs I use to furnish some of my projects—they have some fabulous room designs!"

Two days later, Cassandra called Lori. "I'd love to see those catalogs you told me about at the WIRE meeting. Can I treat you to a coffee?" Shortly after their one-on-one meeting, Lori had an opportunity for Cassandra's firm to bid on a job she had been hired to design. Cassandra's firm won the project and Lori became not only a client, but a true Champion for Cassandra, introducing her to other designers and opportunities.

Cassandra enjoyed meeting new people, and she recalls how motivated she felt after she landed her first client through networking! She sees Bess and Monica sitting at a table in the corner, and wanders over to say hello. "I am going to an amazing event next week, hosted by WIRE," she tells the younger women. "I'd like to bring you both with me and introduce you to some of the heavy hitters in our field." Bess and Monica realize that Cassandra is something special—a true Champion!

I would say I hope you don't encounter any Castoffs at a networking event, but realistically, (sigh!) you'll run across at least one Castoff at every networking event. Remember, every Castoff you encounter takes time away from meeting Champions! The more efficiently you deal with them, the more time you can devote to building productive relationships with your Champions.

Just what makes someone a Champion? Not all Champions are Champions for all people—everyone has their own specific goals for networking—but each Champion has a few things in common:

- **A Champion is a person who will support you.**
- **A Champion is someone who will help you further yourself professionally and personally.**
- **A Champion is waiting for YOU!**

So how do you know someone you have met is a Champion? The Champions are not always obvious. Nor are Champions always Champions when you first meet them.

Let's say you're introduced to a couple of people from a company you may like to work with. After the initial introduction, what's the next move?

## Cultivate the Relationship

Begin with an evaluation. The first move in the process of evaluating a potential Champion is to cultivate the relationship. Cultivating the relationship means doing what is necessary to get to the opportunity to spend time with the target Champion.

But before you can begin to cultivate the relationship, you need to be introduced!

### *The Introduction*

Of course, the easiest way is to ask a mutual acquaintance for an introduction. LinkedIn can be a good tool for discovering common points of contact, or if that doesn't work, try making an announcement at your networking group. Many groups reserve time for members to stand up and announce a specific goal for the week or the month; state the name of the person you wish to meet and see if your networking colleagues can help make it happen.

If you do score an introduction, make it count! Remember the exercise we did earlier on researching our targets when we filled out a Contact Preparation Worksheet? We organized the information we know about our target contact, and more importantly, we identified what we can offer that target. Before you're introduced, prepare by reviewing your notes. Know the basics, and be able to express clearly and directly how you can help the target contact. By having your ducks in a row before you meet, you have a better chance of making a strong impression, which may lead to a fruitful relationship with a Champion.

While introductions may be the easiest and most direct way of meeting someone, sometimes finding that mutual link proves impossible. In that case, what do you do? Introduce yourself! Say it with me..."Introduce myself!" These two words may provoke a fight-or-flight impulse in some of us! But assuming the fight would only be with yourself and flight would be fruitless, resist both and focus on how you can introduce yourself to the target contact.

Everyone is familiar with the saying "breaking the ice" or "ice breaker" when it comes to starting a conversation. I don't know where the phrase comes from, but it makes me think of renegade ice cubes falling from the refrigerator door, shattering as they hit the kitchen floor. Face it, that's how some of our initial encounters with potential Champions sometimes feel. With a little practice, though, it doesn't have to be that way. With the C'crets, you can turn a random ice-breaker into a well-planned, expertly executed "Conversation Catalyst." Let's take a look at some ways to do that.

### *Conversation Catalyst: the Compliment*

One of the easiest Conversation Catalysts to employ is the compliment. It could be as simple as "I love those shoes" or "The article highlighting your business last month was intriguing!" A compliment is hard to resist! Unfortunately, sometimes accepting a compliment is harder than giving one. Because you need to know how to both give *and* receive them, let's take a look at how to graciously accept a compliment.

Picture this: Leanne arrives at an event in a stunning, turquoise blue dress. I don't know Leanne, but walk up to her and say, "Wow, I really like that dress—the color is fabulous!"

Leanne responds, "Oh, I got this on sale. It's probably too late in the season for a sleeveless dress, but I do like the color."

While this response may start a brief conversation—which will peter out quickly if we don't find something else to talk about—a better response from Leanne would have been a simple "thank you." When we are self-effacing about our attire, we run the risk of subliminally conveying the message that we don't think much of ourselves, or, by extension, the work we do.

A direct and simple "thank you!" shows that we have confidence in our abilities and that we take responsibility for our decisions, even the simple ones, like dressing ourselves. The paradox here is that most people dress a certain way in order to garner favorable attention; why reject it when it comes?

I challenge you to notice how you—and those around you—respond to a compliment. Do you say "thank you," or give an apology or excuse? It may be such an ingrained habit that you don't even notice when you respond in a negative way. Initially, it may feel awkward to stop after a simple "thanks!" Practice. Accepting a compliment well can be learned, and through repetition, it will replace the old habit of deflecting praise or admiration. Confidence is contagious. Once you decide how you want others to view you in your stunning turquoise blue dress—as a strong, confident person rather than someone who feels unworthy of a compliment—others will almost subconsciously place faith in you. Let them know you value yourself and your abilities, and they will, too.

### *How Not to Compliment*

Just like with receiving compliments, giving them can sometimes be tricky. The important thing when giving a compliment is to make sure it's appropriate. Certain topics can backfire when you're trying to give a compliment.

As an example: you see Pam for the first time in a few months, and although she hasn't made any reference to it, it's obvious she has lost a lot of weight. A compliment such as, "Pam, you look so thin and healthy!" could be construed positively or negatively. If the compliment is given in front of others, it could make Pam self-conscious, particularly if the others didn't know

Pam when she was overweight. It also implies that Pam was so overweight that it's obvious she has now slimmed down. Either way, your compliment implodes. A better approach would have been to keep it simple and say, "Pam, you look great!" Pam would know what you meant and the others wouldn't know the difference—just the kind of compliment that hits a home run.

An example of an inappropriate compliment that I actually witnessed was, "Hey, Sheri! It's been a long time! Love the boob job!" There are always exceptions, but generally that would not be considered an appropriate compliment at a public event. Of course, it did cause everyone nearby to turn and look!

Back to the "Nice shoes!" compliment. I once complimented a woman on her shoes while in a mixed group of men and women. They were fabulous and I wanted to tell her so! The men, making fun, began complimenting each other on their shoes. It was really quite funny, and everyone laughed. Note to men: many friendships and business deals have been forged over a great pair of shoes! Women know when they are wearing a fabulous pair of shoes and are receptive to other women who recognize a great pair when they see one. So, joke all you want; we will be laughing all the way to the bank. You know, the one that happens to be next door to the shoe store!

### *Conversation Catalyst: Current Events*

I always recommend that before you attend a networking event, spend a few minutes getting up to speed on current events. Ideally, you should be able to participate in a conversation on the topics of sports, news stories and pop culture. Not all of these topics may be your cup of tea, but because the small talk in groups so often focuses on them, it's necessary at least to know the headlines. While standing in a group of four or five, you don't want to be the sole individual who doesn't contribute to the conversation. Or worse yet, you don't want to be the person who, thinking he's making a valid contribution, says something off-kilter that disrupts the flow and makes others uncomfortable. Remember how awkward the Coconut was, talking about something irrelevant to your conversation? The only difference is that the Coconut was not invited to the conversation. Awkwardness does not discriminate! If you join the conversation, you need to contribute in an acceptable way.

Now, other networking gurus tout the first rule of networking as "listening." I don't disagree in general, but I do believe you must actively participate in a conversation: that means *speaking* as well as listening. Chatting about which celebrity is in rehab or pregnant, or about the manager of the local NFL team who just got fired, may not be your first choice of conversational fodder, but these topical and sometimes trite stories give people a common platform, a non-threatening way to interact and take stock of one another. By knowing your news of the day, you give others in a networking setting a way to know you a little bit, too.

It's especially important to be current on local news stories, and here's a good example why: in July of 2012, I was heading to downtown Kansas City to conduct a networking class for a group of lawyers. The city was hosting the Major League All Star game that week and the entire metropolitan area was abuzz with baseball! Flags lined the streets welcoming thousands of visitors to the city, and fans crowded into restaurants and bars wearing their team jerseys. Cops stood outside directing the traffic, and I had to park a few blocks away because the street in front of the lawyers' building was blocked off. We were in the heart of baseball mania.

I stepped into the elevator with one other woman and two men, all lawyer types. Not being one to ride in awkward silence, I commented that it was pretty exciting for Kansas City to host the Big Game! The men nodded in agreement, but the woman looked at me and said, "What game?" Had this conversation taken place at a networking event, this woman would have had the same effect as a Coconut—bringing the conversation to an awkward halt!

Be aware of what's going on in the world—even if you know just enough to nod in agreement or express disagreement appropriately.

### *Conversation Catalyst: the Common Cause*

Our initial reaction when meeting someone is to reach out to shake hands, and sometimes you'll notice that part of them has become real estate for their favorite causes: colorful rubberized bracelets stamped with the name of a charitable organization, or a lapel pin in the shape of a ribbon or the American flag. You may recognize the cause; maybe you support it yourself, or you may even have some personal connection to it. If so, it's appropriate to comment on it. Doing so may lead to the discovery that you both support the same organizations or have had similar experiences, and this could be the catalyst to forge a strong bond between you and the other person. If you are sincere about your conviction, it may entice the other person to cultivate a relationship with you because people like to associate with others of like mind.

A word of caution: common causes may serve as a catalyst to a conversation, but they may also evoke strong emotions. Broach the topic carefully and evaluate the situation to see if further conversation about the common cause is appropriate.

### *Conversation Catalyst: the Colleague in Common*

Nothing binds people together like discovering they know people in common. Indeed, it's one of the foundations of networking, and occurs frequently at all networking events. How many times have people asked you, "Do you know so-and-so?" and when you reply "yes," it's as if a vine has sprouted, leading to many other Colleagues in Common. Suddenly you and your contact are on a quest to find out everyone you know in common and how you each know them.

It's human nature to judge each other, to some degree, by the company we keep. Following that vine of interconnections gives people a good incentive to cultivate a relationship with you, or, sometimes, to not pursue a relationship with you, depending on the nature of their relationship with the people you know in common. Let's look at a couple of scenarios.

You see from her name tag that Cindy West works for Directions, Inc.

"Hello Cindy!" you say. Cindy is one of your target contacts, and you're eager to finally meet her in person. "I know a couple of people who work at Directions. Do you know Brent North?"

Cindy hesitates. "Yes," she says, her eyes shifting away from your face, "I know him." She doesn't volunteer any more information.

By reading Cindy's body language, you pick up that Brent and Cindy may not be on good terms; or maybe for some reason Cindy prefers not to be associated with Brent. Generally, with a curt response like this, it's best not to elaborate or continue the conversation about Brent. Cindy is uncomfortable for some reason—and it may be a good one—but you have no way of knowing why.

Now, let's revisit the same scenario, only this time Cindy answers without hesitation. "Yeah, I know Brent! What a fun guy! Great guy to work with!" Clearly, this is a much more positive response and bodes well as a catalyst for continued conversation.

Alternatively, Cindy may respond with enthusiasm about Brent, but turn the tables on you by asking how you know him. Even if he is a close personal friend, be aware that your conversation is taking place in the business realm, and you still need to observe the conventions of small talk appropriate to a business setting. Blurting out, "I met Brent in rehab a few years ago. He is the nicest person! I still see him at our weekly AA meetings," may be the truth, but it's not something you ought to share at a networking event. Aside from making the conversation awkward, you may be revealing information that Brent does not want to share with his colleagues.

Sometimes having a Colleague in Common turns out to be nothing more than wishful thinking on the part of your contact. Have you ever been in a conversation with someone, perhaps discussing companies you have an interest in, and every time you mention a company he immediately says he knows someone there? Yet even though he seems to know everyone, he doesn't know anyone well enough to get you the introduction you'd like? Later, when you do manage to talk to some of the people he mentioned, they have no idea who he is! This may be one of those instances when a potential Champion morphs into a Castoff: he keeps talking, but you've stopped listening and can only see the lips moving—a sure sign he's a Collagen.

The best way to navigate the Colleagues in Common is by not volunteering too much information. Be the dominant listener and look for cues that reveal how well—or not—this person knows your Colleague in Common. And if you don't know the Colleague in Common well, don't pretend to. While it's human nature to want to build bonds with others by finding these common threads, they'll snap quickly if you profess to know someone better than you do. Don't name-drop, and don't hint at a familiarity that doesn't exist. If you claim to know a Colleague in Common, make sure that Colleague in Common knows you, too.

Not following these guidelines can have some embarrassing results, as I witnessed in person. Standing in line one day to register for a networking program, I overheard two women in front of me introducing themselves to each other.

"Hi, Betsy, I'm Janet," said one, reading her neighbor's name tag. "I see you work for Black Mountain. I know Ted McGrath, your company CEO. Great guy!"

Betsy smiled and after a moment's hesitation, she replied, "Great! Then you should say hi to him. He's standing right behind you."

Janet blushed furiously. It was clear that other than his name, she had no idea who Ted McGrath was. She implied a relationship that didn't exist and it backfired.

Having Colleagues in Common fosters camaraderie and accelerates the conversation in a positive way; stretching the truth and being caught name-dropping kills not only the conversation, but a potential relationship as well.

♛♛♛

So now that you have the conversation rolling, what next? Don't worry! The C'crets won't leave you hanging!

In the next chapter, we will uncover the C'crets: must-do strategies you need to practice at every opportunity in order to cultivate your relationships while searching for a Champion.

**C'crets in action** \sē-krits in ack-shən\ noun, pl:
a system of turning NOTworking into NETworking

# 4 The C′crets in Action

In this section I will introduce you to the meat of the C'crets, including the seven essential C'crets you should practice at every networking event you attend. Doing so will increase the productivity of your networking time and make the networking experience much more enjoyable!

## C'cret #1: CLARIFY YOUR CAREER

At some point early in the conversation, you are sure to hear the networking equivalent of "What's your sign?" I'm talking about the inevitable "So what do you do?" Some people take this as a cue to fumble around for a business card, which honestly gives me the impression you have to look at your business card to know what you do! A much better response when asked this question is to ANSWER it! This is your moment; have a clear, direct statement ready. You know what you do. Now it's time to let others know it, too.

Following are a few options on how to answer this perennial question.

### *Option #1—A Good Answer*

You can answer by stating where you work—especially if you want to cut the conversation short!

Imagine someone has just complimented you. The compliment makes you feel good and fuels your interest in your conversation partner; you want to know more about her so you inquire, "What do you do?"

The bubbly person who caught your attention answers: "I work at Sprint."

What does that tell you? NOTHING!! Sometimes we fall into the trap of thinking all we have to do is state our company's name and people will know what we do for a living. But there are very few instances where the company name explains all the jobs contained within the company!

Slowly, the good feelings at the start of the conversation begin to ebb. Why? Because now you have to *work* at the conversation. Suddenly it becomes your job to ferret out the very information you were asking for, which causes your friendly curiosity to take a nosedive. After all, if a person isn't interested enough in her job to tell you what she does, why should you be?

### *Option # 2—A Better Answer*

Now let's revisit the previous example, only this time the person answers, "I work at Sprint. I'm a budget analyst in the mobile division." Does this make you feel any better? Yes, because now you have information that tells you something about that person. You understand she works in budgeting, not in tech support, and you may deduce that she is more analytical than technical. (A small voice in your head still wants to ask why your phone does that black screen thing, but you resist...) This brief job description gives just a little more detail to *clarify* and give life to the potential direction of the conversation.

### *Option #3—A Knock'em-Dead Answer*

The example above suggested a perfectly suitable answer to the question, "What do you do?" In many situations, this will be the best you can produce. But if you've done your homework before attending a networking event—built your worksheet, zeroed in on your target contacts and gathered information about what they do in their job—there's an even better alternative. Use what you've learned—either about the contact himself, or the company he works for—to tailor a specific response. Following is an example of how it works.

From reading the business section of the local newspaper (as a savvy networker, you never miss it), you learn that Company RE is on a roll, buying up real estate all over town. As someone who sells commercial insurance, worker's comp, and employee benefits, you understand the potential of gaining Company RE as a client. You make Joyce, their VP of property management, a target contact for your next real estate networking event. Now, after you've prepared your contact sheet, shined your shoes and arrived on time, you find yourself in a crowded room shaking hands with Joyce when suddenly that old familiar question pops up: "What do you do?" Here are a few ways you can answer Joyce:

"I sell insurance." (Not bad.)

"I'm in the commercial insurance industry." (Better.)

"I provide real estate investors options for their commercial insurance." (Bingo!)

Which answer will Joyce find most intriguing? Clearly, it's the one that connects your job with her needs. You've provided information that's relevant to Joyce and her company, which will make her more apt to remember you after the event. When you follow up with a one-on-one appointment, you'll be able to share some of the options for commercial insurance and perhaps secure some business, all because you put a little effort into crafting a thoughtful response!

NEVER assume that someone knows what you do. Unless your title is President of the United States, you should plan to clarify your job or what your company does. Work on an answer to the question "What do you do?" now so that you have a clear, understandable and meaningful answer later when you need it.

## *TLAs*

Every type of communication today contains several TLAs. If we were talking in person right now, you'd probably be nodding your head while thinking to yourself, "What's a TLA?"

Most of us respond this way when confronted with an unfamiliar TLA because though inundated with TLAs, we're afraid of looking uninformed when we don't know what they mean.

(Reader: "Enough already! What's a TLA??!

Author: "FYI, a TLA is a Three Letter Acronym.")

If I introduce myself as a CPA to someone attuned to accounting, he'll nod his head with acknowledgment. But if, for example, I introduce myself to Bob, who has no idea what a CPA does, he'll look at me like a DIH (Deer in Headlights)! People unfamiliar with my profession may or may not ask me additional questions to better understand what I do; if they don't, we both potentially miss out on a good contact. And who's at fault when this happens? I am! As in the previous example with Joyce, it's not Bob's responsibility to play detective and sleuth out the particulars of my job; I need to communicate that clearly.

Now what if I introduce myself as a CPA that specializes in helping small businesses with their accounting and tax needs? Even if my target isn't sure what a CPA is, he will know what services I provide, which is exactly the information I am trying to convey.

♛♛♛

Take a minute to write your "What do you do?" script. Be honest, be creative and be concise! When you're through, read it out loud, then test it on a few people who may not know exactly what you do. Do they have a better understanding of your job after hearing your "What do you do?" script? Revise until they do!

**What I do:** ______________________________

______________________________

______________________________

______________________________

______________________________

______________________________

______________________________

______________________________

______________________________

## C'cret #2: CONFIDENCE

When talking with someone about what you do, there is one word, one attitude that you must keep in the forefront—CONFIDENCE. Like we said before: confidence is contagious! If you are confident about what you do, that confidence is transferred to others: by being sure of yourself and your abilities, others will place their confidence in you, too.

There are many ways of showing confidence: a firm handshake, erect posture, appropriate eye contact, engaging speech. Taken together, all these things are a powerful means of relaying your confidence. More importantly, though, they need to be rooted in a confidence of your professional abilities. Following is a good example why.

Recently I attended a Chamber of Commerce event where new members were invited to introduce themselves. Dan stood up, introduced himself, and explained he had just purchased a printing franchise. He looked directly at the crowd as he spoke and didn't stammer or trip over his words. So far, so good. Then he continued: "I don't know anything about printing, never spent a day of my life involved with it before this. There's a lot of technology involved that I'm unfamiliar with. And I'm not sure about the abilities of my current staff. But I had some capital to invest and I've always dreamed of owning my own company. I'm determined to make this work!"

Now it's possible that Dan was nervous and didn't know what to say. But having witnessed this in person, I got the impression that Dan wasn't so much anxious as he was unprepared, that he had arrived expecting to be introduced without realizing he would be facing the entire Chamber, fumbling for something to say about his new business. He had drive and motivation, and showed little fear of the risk of starting something new; but those qualities paled beside his admission that he didn't know what he was doing as a printer. Because he lacked confidence in his professional abilities, he made it impossible for anyone else to have confidence in him either.

Confidence is essential in networking. Following are a few ways to put it into action.

### *Have Confidence in Your Service or Product*

First of all, be confident of what you represent. If you aren't sure of yourself, nobody will be!

Being confident will look different for everyone. The trick is to appear confident without coming across as arrogant. Confidence is not bragging about yourself or your business; it's not putting other people down or casting rival businesses in a bad light. Confidence is being passionate about what you do, and being a conduit of that energy for others. Let me give you an example:

Rob owns a company and is interested in doing something to increase business, but he's not sure what that "something" looks like. At a business networking meeting, he meets Jake, who owns a marketing agency. Let's eavesdrop on their conversation.

**Rob:** *My business is growing, but not at the pace I'd like it to. I'm not totally convinced the marketing people know what they are doing. They're always wanting me to change my logo, do a zillion different promotions, start some trendy new social media page, but what I really want is to just keep it simple. I don't trust these guys with my checkbook!*

**Jake:** *I hear you! I think it's interesting that so many businesses jump into a marketing plan that is put in place for them. Not every owner wants to participate in all the details of a marketing plan, but I think the marketing plans with the best results usually have the owner on board. Successful marketing is an extension of the owner's beliefs and goals for his company.*

**Rob:** *So you're saying I need to feel comfortable with the marketing message?*

**Jake:** *Yes, but more importantly, the message should complement the company philosophy and culture. The message should not stick out where it's recognized as a "marketing" push.*

**Rob:** *I like that idea. Would you have time to come visit our company and let me bounce some ideas around?*

It is very clear that Rob has confidence in Jake. This conversation could have easily gone a different way. Non-confident responses could have looked like this:

**Jake:** *Whoa! Not all of us are bad guys! I've done some of the best promotions for XYZ company and they don't think I'm a jerk!*

or this:

**Jake:** *Wow, sounds like you got ahold of some bad eggs! Who is your marketing firm? I could come in and revamp your marketing plan for you.*

The first response is very defensive and a bit arrogant. It doesn't offer any ideas or solutions, just self-promotion.

Like the first response, the second fails to offer ideas on how Rob's marketing could be improved. It focuses on the failures of his current marketing firm without giving any reason why Rob would want to hire Jeff to "revamp" his marketing plan. All Rob will think of is the expense of redoing what the "marketing guys" should have done.

### *The Clutch*

Another aspect of confidence is the CLUTCH. The clutch is your handshake, and it's one of your first opportunities to establish confidence in a new target.

How does the clutch create confidence? A weak handshake can infer meekness, a lack of willingness to "put yourself out there," while a strong, firm handshake reflects a positive attitude, and a belief in your abilities. Firm doesn't mean aggressive—you don't shake the person's arm so hard that the arm comes out of the socket!

One more thing about the firm handshake; some people like to do the two-handed grip. This is when someone grips your hand as if he were going to shake it, but instead closes his other hand over yours and then pumps your arm. The two-handed grip is not appropriate for someone you've just met; it's best reserved for people with whom you are familiar, related to in some way, or have a strong emotional connection to. I like to call this the Grandma Grip!

## C'cret #3: CAPITALIZE!

A third way to convey confidence is to CAPITALIZE your conversation. Imagine what your speech would look like if it were written dialogue. Do you EMPHASIZE certain words through INFLECTION or a change in the TONE of your voice? Whole episodes of sitcoms have been devoted to monotone speakers and with good reason. Monotone speech is lifeless; confidence cannot exist without a degree of enthusiasm. Let that show in your voice.

Look at the following snippets of conversation. Which would you prefer to be a part of? (Read this part out loud to get the full effect!)

*"We had a surprise party for Megan last night. She came in the house and we all yelled surprise."*

or,

*"We had a SURPRISE party for Megan last night! She came in the house and we all yelled SURPRISE!!"*

While emailing in all CAPS is considered yelling at the recipient and poor email etiquette, talking in capital letters is ENERGETIC. Your voice inflection makes all the difference in understanding the context of what you are saying. Has anyone ever told you something in a monotone voice or without punctuation or emphasis, and you weren't quite sure if what they were saying was a good thing or bad? Here's a short exercise to illustrate what I mean. Read the following sentences with a positive tone; then repeat with a negative tone:

*"I spoke to my landlord today and the replacement floor is going to be tile."*

*"It snowed five inches today."*

Depending on your emphasis of certain words—by capitalizing them through your speech or not—you convey a different meaning through use of the same sentence. Imagine calling a pet dog without any inflection in your voice; does it "recognize" its own name? It's tempting to think your dog understands you when you speak, but generally it's the tone and CAPTIALIZATION of certain words that it recognizes. If you have a pet dog, try out the following two sentences—first with and then without CAPITALIZATION.

*"Harry, drop the shoe."*

*"Poppy, let's go for a ride."*

When someone talks without capitalizing his ideas, it comes across like he is trying to stay in the background of the conversation, that he is afraid to put himself out there. It's as if he doesn't really want others to listen to what he is saying. And they won't. Instead, what they'll "hear" is a lack of confidence. CAPITALIZE effectively to convey CONFIDENCE and to ensure your message is received accurately.

## C'cret #4: CONVERSATION

Often at networking events, several representatives from the same industry will be present. Sometimes these are friendly competitors, other times they compete fiercely with one another. Regardless of who is in attendance, it's important to watch what you say in conversation.

Now I've been stressing the importance of being prepared, and presumably you will be walking into your next networking event with some knowledge of your target contacts. Use this information wisely and know when to practice discretion. It's imperative that you not ask a question or make a comment that could be damaging to the contact if overheard by a competitor. For example, when I researched Mr. Todd Albright, Financial Officer of Growing Companies, Inc., I learned that the company was in acquisition mode and expanding rapidly. I see Mr. Albright at a networking event just as I had planned and—after having spent time getting prepared and practicing the C'crets—I now find myself enjoying a productive, one-on-one conversation with him. I'd like to let him know that I'm aware of his company's recent acquisitions, and that I have some helpful ideas for his accounting department. I could say one of two things:

**Choice #1**: *"I've noticed your company has a strong appetite for acquisitions. I would imagine that merging the processes and procedures would be the most challenging part of your job. I've worked with several companies just after they made acquisitions, and I know it can be very stressful blending the companies together!"*

**Choice #2:** *"I've noticed your company has a strong appetite for acquisitions. It looks like acquiring ABC Co. or LMN Co. would be the next logical next step for you. I would imagine that merging the processes and procedures would be the most challenging part of your job. I've worked with several companies just after they made acquisitions, and I know it can be very stressful blending the companies together!"*

Both choices contain the information I want to convey. They are actually almost identical; however, choice #2 has one sentence that should be saved for a private, one-on-one conversation. If a competitor is nearby and he overhears bits and pieces of the conversation, he may deduce that Growing Companies is interested in acquiring ABC Co. or LMN Co. If this is indeed the case, having a competitor know this (or even just guess it) could be harmful to my contact's company.

Conversation can work FOR you as well. Here's a real life example from one of my networking experiences:

I was relaying a funny story to Cassie, a new contact, about how I got to meet Sir Elton John.

"It was tax season," I said, "and I was up late working with the tv on to keep me company. It was tuned to a PBS telethon; the announcer said they had ten pairs of first-row tickets for an upcoming concert with Sir Elton John with a chance to meet him in person! I was so excited it took me a minute to realize I was punching in the phone number on my calculator. When I finally found the phone under a pile of papers and called in, I won a pair of tickets! The funny thing was that half the tickets that night were won by other CPAs who were up working late, too! By the time of the concert, I was eight months pregnant; when I met Sir Elton, he reached over to give me a big hug. Between his stomach and mine, it was very awkward!"

By making my story compelling (another conversational C'cret we will address later), I was able to engage Cassie's interest and begin to forge a bond with her. Better yet, I was aware that Margaret, another of my target contacts, was chatting with a small group of people next to us. I had hoped to subtly catch Margaret's attention with my story, and it worked. She leaned over and said, "I couldn't help but overhear you. I'm a huge fan of Sir Elton John—what a great story! And you said you're a

CPA? That's got to be the best CPA story I've heard!" From there, I was able to speak with Margaret and make an excellent contact!

When employing conversation to attract target contacts, be conscious of WHAT you are saying, WHERE you are saying it and WHO is within earshot!

## C'cret #5: CARDS

One of my favorite questions from audience members during my networking presentations is, "When do I hand someone my business card?"

Cards are both a blessing and a curse when it comes to networking. Yes, they are an effective means of sharing contact information, but too often when asked where we work or what we do, we reach for a business card instead of replying with a direct and thoughtful answer. The card becomes a substitute for talking. Instead of taking these questions as an opportunity to spark a conversation, we short-circuit the bonding opportunity by passing along our business card that, without a genuine human connection to give it meaning, will most likely end up in the trash. What's worse, when we let our cards do our talking for us, we give the impression that we have tidily dealt with a fellow networker and are relieved to move on to someone with more potential. It's never right to monopolize someone's time at an event, but do take the time to verbally communicate with potential targets. Use business cards as a supplement to your introduction, not a surrogate for that introduction. Talk first, then give your business card as a way to reinforce the relationship you have begun to cultivate.

Cards are convenient when you meet a potential Champion that you'd like to meet one-on-one, but hand them out sparingly! Give your cards only to people you really want to be in contact with. If you're walking around with cards in your hand and passing them out to everyone you see, you'll most likely later find yours in the "carpet" of business cards that line the floor or parking lot.

Invest in a business card holder that fits in your pocket or purse. (Occasionally a unique business card holder embossed with a college emblem, an association or just a fun design can be a conversation catalyst.) Ideally, when you meet someone you would like to connect with again, take your card out of the holder and write a quick note on it; a simple "I'll call you for coffee," or "Great talking with you!" will help set you apart after the event, when the "sorting of the business cards" ritual takes place.

## C'cret #6: CULINARY

The culinary is the perfect segue, a time-honored means of transitioning from an introduction to an invitation to meet one-on-one. Why CULINARY? Because we all eat and drink. Take the opportunity to invite your contact to coffee or lunch to continue your conversation.

"I'm really enjoying talking with you! Can I invite you to coffee next week so that we can continue our conversation?" you can suggest.

Or, "I know I shouldn't  monopolize your time here, let's get together next week for coffee. Here is my card, may I have yours? I'll give you a buzz next week!"

Many networking events can be noisy, making it difficult to have a conversation. If this is the case you might say, "It's difficult to carry on a conversation in here! Let's pick a day next week to meet for coffee—someplace where we can hear each other!"

## C'cret #7: COMPELLING

This last C'cret—to be COMPELLING—is one that audiences usually say is the hardest to master. However difficult, it can also be the most interesting C'cret of all.

A compelling story or comment is one that stays with people after you leave. Have you ever been in a group where one person is telling a story while everyone else listens raptly, fully engaged? Where the Cucumber isn't looking bored, the Collagen is momentarily silent, and the Coconut knows better than to drop in? The narrator of the story could be recounting a personal anecdote, or a story she heard, or simply talking about a vacation on the horizon. Being COMPELLING entices people to engage with you, remember you and continue to speak with you! Compelling doesn't mean the story is earth-shattering, or that it contains an "aha!" moment; even ordinary stories can be told in a compelling way.

*How* you tell a story is as important as the story itself. Are you passionate, humorous, vibrant and/or dramatic when you tell a story or recount an event?

One way to become more compelling is to learn from others. For example, pay attention when people talk about someone they've just met. What is it that compelled that person to remember their new acquaintance, and better yet, want to tell you about him?

The stories we tell other networkers don't have to focus on our business. Remember my story about Sir Elton John? It resonated with Margaret because it revealed a common interest, one that had nothing to do with our work. Sometimes, stories of a more personal nature are safer in a networking setting because you don't run the risk of divulging sensitive business information by accident.

What is interesting about you or the experiences you've had? Start collecting a cache of interesting, compelling anecdotes you feel comfortable sharing, stories you've learned to tell well. For example, have you been on a recent trip to an unusual place? Do you have an interesting hobby? Have you encountered someone famous or infamous? What funny or interesting predicaments have you been in?

Think about what makes *you* compelling. Next, what compels you to remember others?

After coming up with one or more compelling stories, the next step is to work them into your conversation. This part is a little tougher! The best way is to look for an opening. Don't try to shoehorn in a story that has no connection to the conversation, but don't wait for the perfect moment, either. Be bold. There may not always be an opening, but if there is—take it!

I'll give you an example. I was standing in a small group of people at an event, all of whom I had just met for the first time. During our small talk, someone mentioned he had been at the Bon Jovi concert the night before. One of the women said she wished she could have met him—he was her favorite performer. The conversation could have easily headed in another direction, but I saw my opening and piped up: "I took my four-year old son to the concert last night. He's my little rock star magnet, and sure enough, Bon Jovi came over and gave him a guitar pick and the song list! He even scooped up my son and held him for a moment. That's when I reached over and touched Bon Jovi's hair!"

While this story is very low on the totem pole of achieving world peace, it is nonetheless *entertaining* and *compelling*. So much so that a month later when I saw one of the networkers at another event she jokingly asked if she could take my son to an upcoming concert! Providing a conversation catalyst that is humorous and compelling is a good way to get people to remember you. That's the goal. Just don't overdo it, and don't overshadow or one-up someone else's story—you'll make others feel uncomfortable, and you will come across as insincere.

One other thing to remember: compelling stories should be for all ears. Be careful not to be offensive. Expect to be overheard while talking—people are prone to eavesdropping, especially at networking events. This can work to your advantage when you're recounting a funny or interesting story; someone may feel compelled to introduce himself!

*On the following page, jot down some interesting places you've been, things you've experienced or people you've met, then pick a couple to turn into a story. Make sure they are engaging but concise.*

**Places:**________________________________________

**Experiences:**____________________________________

**People:** ________________________________________

♛♛♛

Now that you've met your target contacts, conversed with them, arranged follow-up meetings and have actually gotten to know them—what's next?

Even after going through all of the recommendations described in this book, most of these prospects will not end up as your Champions. As you increase your networking activity, you'll meet many people. Some will be Castoffs and some will be nice people whose agenda simply does not match up with your own.

The Champions are a rarer find. You'll recognize a Champion based on his interest in you and his willingness to help you grow your business. True Champions love to connect people and will waste no time doing so. They won't make you feel indebted to them although you will feel the urge to reciprocate! True Champions will inform you of other networking events or groups they consider worthwhile. These insights can be priceless—make every effort to attend.

The Champions are the gold at the end of the networking rainbow! Well-positioned Champions can provide you with all the business or referrals you need to grow your business. As a bonus, some of your relationships with Champions may develop beyond the work stage and develop into genuine friendships.

## Honorary Mention Champions

Here are a few Champions you'll come across who wear a neon sign touting their willingness to connect others!

### *Cheers*

Remember the old tv show "Cheers?" The characters gathered in a congenial Boston bar "where everyone knows your name." At most networking events, there seems to be someone in the crowd who knows everyone else; he greets people by name, introduces them to each other, and the crowd tends to gravitate toward him. If you don't know him, you should! Even if this person isn't one of your target contacts, go introduce yourself.

### *Conduit*

A current of energy runs through the Conduit and spreads like wildfire to those around him. The Conduit is someone who can walk into a room and electrify the crowd with his dynamic personality. If you're lucky enough to encounter a Conduit, harness some of this energy by introducing yourself. At the very least you will come away from the event pumped up!

### *The Count /Countess*

Counts and Countesses are networking royalty! They weren't born into royalty, they earned the designation based on their willingness to help connect people. The Countess might be someone who retired from a successful business career and now enjoys helping others become successful. The Count may be a "natural" at connecting others, someone who realizes his gift and uses it to help others. Do what you can to get to know them. Ask them for help with meeting your starred contacts. Counts and Countesses thrive on making connections for others. These royalty can provide resources you never even knew existed!

# CONCLUSION

Think of networking as a game on your laptop or tablet. You start the game by choosing a networking event to attend. After successful preparation you move to the second level, in which you have to navigate around the Castoffs. With the Castoffs behind you, the next level challenges you to cultivate relationships with the Contestants. Successful cultivation advances you to the top level where you are surrounded by Champions! Once you reach this final level, you put the C'crets into action to cultivate a relationship with your Champions. The prize? You will have connected with other professionals who share your desire to grow your business. One last C'cret: now that you've found your Champions, strive to be a Champion for others!

I look forward to seeing you at your next networking event!

# Acknowledgments

Possessing the passion to tell a story is not enough to bring it to print. It takes the skills of many professionals. A special thanks to my editor, Amy Woods Butler, who has become a true Champion for my story. Through osmosis, she has become quite a networker in her own right! Special thanks to Michael Morris for bringing the Castoffs to life through his brilliant artwork! Who else would be up at 1 am to share a laugh about my voice recognition mishaps? Thank you to Karen Samuelson for her encouragement, friendship and exemplary proofreading skills! Without you this book would be a punctuation disaster! I don't want to forget to acknowledge two special friends. Malissa Jett has known that I wanted to be an author since we were eight years old, and has encouraged me for the past forty-three years to write. Amy Kemper has been my rock and shares my passion for writing. Thank you for always being available to read my latest manuscript. I love you both. Finally, I would like to thank all of you who have been at my presentations and told me,"You should write a book! This is good stuff!" Well folks, here it is! Enjoy!

# ABOUT THE AUTHOR

The comment most often heard by Debbie is, "*You* can't be a CPA! You have way too much personality!"

Debbie Leonard is indeed a CPA of a different breed. She is the business development partner in the CPA firm of Thill & Leonard, CPAs, LLC, and specializes in business planning, taxation, efficiency implementation and growth strategies. In addition to her CPA, Debbie holds an MBA in Marketing and Finance. She earned her CCIM (Certified Commercial Investment Member) designation and is recognized as an expert in commercial real estate. Despite the alphabet soup of degrees and certifications, marketing and networking are Debbie's true passion.

Debbie is well known among the networking royalty in town. Since facilitating the Home Based Business Connection in the late 80's, and starting the wildly successful Business Referral Alliance (BRA) group in 1992, she has been a vibrant addition to many discussion panels, "lunch & learns" and training seminars on the topics of marketing and networking. Debbie loves to teach and uses humor and a keen insight into human nature to create entertaining lessons that help both beginning and experienced networkers.

Debbie and her family reside in Overland Park, Kansas and are devout Jayhawk fans.

## *Have a networking success story to share?*

**Your story could be highlighted in the upcoming *More C'crets of Networking* or featured on my website, www.networkingqueenpub.com.**

Contact me with your networking stories at **debbie@networkingqueenpub.com**, and visit my website for more networking tips.

Want to have the C'crets of Networking presented in person to your networking group or organization? Visit my website to book a speaking engagement and help others learn the C'crets of Networking, too! Be sure to check out the Calendar of Events for upcoming speaking engagements and networking opportunities.

www.ingramcontent.com/pod-product-compliance
Lightning Source LLC
Chambersburg PA
CBHW071208200326
41519CB00018B/5429